to build a nation

to build a nation

3,000 B.C.	First tribes enter Korea from Manchuria
57	Silla became a state, capital at Kyongju
37	Koguryo became a state, capital at T'onggu
18	Paekche became a state, capital near Seoul
757 A.D.	Silla adopted Chinese governmental system
935	Silla king gave up throne to Koryo
1259	Koryo became vassal state of Mongols
1356	Revolt against Mongols
1392	Yi dynasty established
1394	Capital moved to Seoul
1419-50	Reign of Sejong, "Golden Age," Korean alphabet, hangul, invented, many books printed
1568	Complete control of the state by Confucianists assured
1592-1596	Japanese invasion under Hideyoshi

to build a nation

1627	Invasion by Manchus. Korea a vassal state until 1895. Fear of foreign powers so great that the king enforced strict isolation until Korea became known as the "Hermit Kingdom."
1784	Christianity introduced by Korean converted in China
1884	Treaty signed with the U.S. establishing diplomatic and commercial relations. Korea's first trade treaty with a Western power.
1884	First Protestant missionary entered Korea
1894-95	Sino-Japanese War. China relinquished suzeranity over Korea.
1905	Treaty of Portsmouth signed, ending Russo-Japanese War
1910-1945	Annexation and occupation by Japan

to build a nation

1919	Declaration of Independence signed by 33 Korean patriots, non-violent revolt against Japanese rule, leading to establishment of Provisional Government of Korea in exile
1945 (Aug. 15)	Liberation
1948 (Aug. 14)	Establishment of the Republic of Korea with Syngman Rhee as the first president of South Korea
1950 (June 25)	Outbreak of the Korean War
1953 (July 27)	The Armistice Agreement Signed at Panmunjom
1953 (Aug. 16)	The Republic of Korea and the United States of America signed a Mutual Security Agreement
1960 (Apr. 19-20)	The April 19 Student Revolution overthrows Syngman Rhee
1960 (June 19)	State Visit of President Dwight D. Eisenhower to Korea
1961 (May 16)	The May 16 Military Revolution

to build a nation

1963 (Oct. 15)	Election of Park Chung-hee as President of Third Republic
1965 (May 16-27)	State Visit of President and Madame Park Chung-hee to the United States
1966 (Oct. 31-Nov. 2)	State Visit of President Lyndon B. Johnson and Mrs. Johnson to Korea
1967 (Feb. 9)	U. S.-ROK Status of Forces Agreement goes into effect
1967 (May 3)	President Park Chung-hee re-elected by majority vote, winning over nearest rival by 1.16 million votes
1967 (July 1)	Second inauguration of President Park Chung-hee
1968 (Apr. 17-18)	President Park meets with President Johnson in Hawaii

to build

by PARK CHUNG HEE

PUBLISHED BY

acropolis books

WASHINGTON, D.C. 20009

a nation

*Namdae-mun, or the South Gate, was originally built
as one of the main gates of the city wall of Seoul in 1396.
Rebuilt in 1448, the present structure is one of the most
ancient architectural remnants of the beginning of
the Yi Dynasty, the last dynasty in Korea (1392-1910).
Today, it is found in the heart of busy downtown Seoul,
surrounded by new modern high-rise buildings.*

ACROPOLIS BOOKS LTD.
*Colortone Building, 2400 17th St., N.W.
Washington, D. C. 20009*

Printed in the United States of America by
Colortone Creative Graphics Inc., *Washington, D. C. 20009*

*Type set in English
by Colortone Typographic Division, Inc.*

Design by Design and Art Studio 2400, Inc.

Library of Congress Catalog Number 70-148049

Standard Book No. 87491-136-2

6498

The Korean flag symbolizes much of the thought philosophy and mysticism of the Orient. The symbol, and sometimes the flag itself, is called Tae Geuk.

Depicted on the flag is a circle divided equally and locked in perfect balance. The upper (red) section represents the Yang and the lower (blue) section the Um. These two opposites express the dualism of the universe. There are heaven and earth, day and night, dark and light, construction and destruction, masculine and feminine, active and passive, heat and cold, plus and minus, and so on.

The central thought in the Tae Geuk indicates that while there is a constant movement within the sphere of infinity, there are also balance and harmony. As a simple example, kindness and cruelty may be taken into consideration. If parents are kind to a child, it is good; if they are too kind to him, their kindness becomes a form of cruelty, for they spoil and weaken him and may lead him to become a vicious man and a source of disgrace to his ancestors.

Three bars at each corner also carry the ideas of opposite and balance. The three unbroken lines stand for heaven; the opposite three broken lines represent the earth. At the lower left hand of the flag are two lines with a broken line in between. This symbolizes fire. The opposite is the symbol of water.

contents

FOREWORD   13

INTRODUCTION / A Glorious Heritage   18

CHAPTER ONE / Trials and Awakening   32
    The Stormy Wave of Imperialism   32
    Pioneers of Modernization   38
    The Declaration of
        an Independent People   51

CHAPTER TWO / A Devout Will
             to Find Freedom   63
    The Price of Liberation   63
    The Triumph of Conviction   78
    The Long, Thorny Way to Freedom   89

CHAPTER THREE / The Takeoff of
             the 1960's   101
    The Will to Develop   101
    Groundwork for Self-Sufficiency   114
    Efforts Rewarded   124

CHAPTER FOUR / Tides of the Pacific   135
    The Compass of Peace   135
    The Future of Peaceful Coexistence   141
    The Will to Unification   150

CHAPTER FIVE / We Shall Not
                       Give Up Halfway   170
    The Continuing Challenge   170
    The Enhancement of National Identity   181
    The Pride of a Cultured Nation   187

A QUIET REVOLUTION   197

INDEX   209

foreword

The Republic of Korea, the Korean people themselves, their culture, history and traditions were little known to the outside world prior to the outbreak of the Korean War in 1950. It was through this war, which tragically pitted brother against brother, that the eyes of the world were focused upon us. And what image was reflected to the world?—a people only recently liberated from the bonds of imperialism, discouraged and disheartened by the artificial division of their country, poverty-stricken, suffering from the devastation of war; a nation threatened by the continuing menace of communism, dependent almost totally on outside powers for its defense, and with leaders apparently incapable of rescuing the nation from chaos.

Yet, during the last decade dramatic changes have taken place in Korea.

Internationally, the Republic of Korea has truly achieved its independence in its relationship to other nations in the international community. We have established friendly and cooperative relationships with these nations and are no longer completely dependent on others for our defense and well-being.

But even more dramatic have been the changes within our country. Sloughing off their desperation, the Korean people have arisen with a new spirit, a new sense of resolve and purpose to reconstruct their nation, to build a society in which each man may prosper and fulfill himself and may look to the future with hope and confidence.

In 1961 when I, as a military officer, resolved to arise with my colleagues to save the nation from the chaos which threatened to engulf it—a step I took with extreme reluctance, believing that the military should not interfere in political affairs—I realized that our revolution would be successful only if it were a revolution that took root in the minds and hearts of the people.

We were the doctors attempting to save a desperately ill patient, but of course no doctor can be successful unless his patient has a strong will to live. And his future health cannot be maintained unless steps are taken to protect him from the virus that caused his illness.

The first step that needed to be taken was to build a self-reliant economy, to infuse in the people a sense of pride in their ability to accomplish what is now recognized internationally as "a miraculous economic progress" and to make of their nation "a model of developing countries." This we have achieved, but in a sense the particular

The author takes
the oath of office
on his first inauguration
as President of
the Republic of Korea,
on December 17, 1963.

15

achievements—the rise in per capita income, in exports, the construction of industries and expressways—are secondary to the tremendous confidence that has been created, a confidence that we can do whatever we set our hearts on and work hard for.

I took it as my main task, as the leader of the nation during this period, to inspire the confidence and courage of the people to achieve these national goals in a spirit of unity.

In assuming this task I found it necessary to reflect deeply on the history of our nation, on the characteristics of our culture and traditions, and on the capabilities of our people.

I found in my reflections, and share with you in this book, what I feel are the common threads and the unique national spirit that link our past, our present, and our future.

Our past history seems at first glance to be more a record of misfortune than of glory, but we find also in our past a strong inspiration and we value even the misfortunes for the strong sense of determination they have nourished in our people's hearts.

In this sense the accomplishments of Korea in the last decade are grounded firmly in our past, and will lead us to complete the task of rebuilding our nation, to achieve an end to the tragic division of our nation, to secure our defense, and to further develop our economy to the point where all our people may live in freedom, peace, and prosperity.

Our goals, however, are not to be achieved for only our benefit. We intend to be a people and a nation capable of contributing to world peace and prosperity, working together with other nations on a basis of mutual reciprocity and goodwill.

It is my sincere hope that this book, written at the request of Encyclopaedia Britannica, may not only contribute to an increased understanding of Korea by Korea's friends and win their deeper friendship, but will also serve as an inspiration to them.

이 정 희

Park Chung Hee

introduction

a glorious
heritage

Korea's modern liberation from colonialism took place little more than a quarter-century ago. It was even more recently that the Republic of Korea held this nation's first representative election in 1948.

Thus, if the term "newly emerging nation" is applied to all independent nations that were liberated from colonial rule following the end of World War II, Korea undeniably counts as a newly emerging nation. But considering Korea's centuries-old existence as a nation-state, one should realize that Korea is fundamentally different from the majority of what nowadays are called the newly emerging nations, i.e., those transformed for the first time in the present century from a nomadic state or tribal society into a unified country.

In its beginnings Korea was a divided country, split between the kingdoms of Koguryo (37 B.C.-A.D.

*Excavated in the
ancient royal tomb in Kyongju,
the Gold Crown dates
from the Old Silla Dynasty,
5th-6th century.
It is made of cut sheet-gold,
and decorated with
punched dots and numerous spangles and jade.
Height 1 ft. 5-1/2 in.
National Museum of Korea, Seoul.*

19

668), Paekchae (18 B.C.-A.D. 660), and Silla (57 B.C.-A.D. 935). In A.D. 676 the rulers of Silla unified the three kingdoms, and Korea remained as a single nation thereafter. Several titular revolutions took place, however, that toppled corrupt and incompetent dynasties. Silla was replaced by Koryo in 935 and Koryo by the Yi Dynasty in 1392. Except for these instances, Korea has maintained its coherent system as a unified nation-state throughout its history—until it was sundered into north and south sections in 1945.

Taking advantage of Korea's strategic peninsula location in northeast Asia, the peoples of the North Asian hinterland attempted to use Korea as a beachhead for their advance toward the sea. The insular people of Japan, on the other hand, wished to secure Korea as an outpost for their forays onto the continent. Hence, Korea was frequently invaded. Yet during their long history, Koreans have been known as a particularly peace-loving people who never waged a provocative war to invade alien nations.

Minor raids aside, Korea has suffered from nine major invasions in the past 2,000 years. The first attack by the Han dynasty of China (206 B.C.-A.D. 220) went on for several hundred years. Korea was later invaded by the Sui dynasty (589-616), the T'ang dynasty (618-907), once by the Khitan (916-1125), once by the Yuan (1277-1367), twice by Japan, and once by the Ch'ing (1616-1911). The Chinese, the Mongols, the Manchu, and the Japanese all have intruded into Korea for centuries. Whenever they trod on Korean soil, many Koreans were killed and farmland was ravaged.

It might well be surmised that such frequent invasions would have ended the nation's existence or at the least, eroded its national spirit, language and culture. During each invasion thousands of Koreans were slaughtered. Yet their survivors maintained our nation-state intact, both in terms of racial homogeneity and cultural uniqueness. This in itself is a miracle of human history.

Consider the Mongols who once swept across all Asia and into eastern Europe, or the desert Arabs of Islam. Despite rapid expansion and vast domains, both of these nations declined. Compared with them, we have shown a much stronger viability and indomitability. In modern times the government of pre-war imperial Japan made systematic attempts for over 30 years to eliminate Korean unity and culture. Yet in the end the Japanese subversion of Korea's identity proved as ephemeral as raindrops on lotus leaves.

Rather, the ordeals of Korea served as a stimulus, for its people displayed marvelous powers of recuperation. During the Japanese invasion by Hideyoshi — about 380 years ago—the Korean population decreased to four million. According to the census conducted 200 years later, however, during the reign of King Yeongjo (1725-66), the population had recovered to the level of seven million. Today the people of the Republic of Korea alone number 35 million. Add some 15 million in Communist North Korea and the total 50 million demonstrates more than a three-fold increase in the last 60 years. It is likely that the population will increase to 80 million in another 30 years' time.

Cultural creativity and native inventiveness were surely major factors in Korea's stubborn survival. The people of Korea could always derive consolation and pride from their extraordinary, living heritage.

Koreans absorbed diverse strands of Chinese culture. In earlier days Korea imported both her spiritual and material culture from the Han dynasty. During the three-kingdom period, Buddhism as well as T'ang culture were introduced to Korea. The Koryo dynasty of ancient Korea first assimilated Sung dynasty culture, on which succeeding generations blended influences from the Yuan, Ming and Ch'ing dynasties. Korea refined these Chinese cultures, in many cases developing standards higher than those of the originals.

Silla and Koryo not only produced eminent Buddhist leaders of international reputation, but also reinforced Buddhist theory. Later Koreans of the Yi dynasty (1392-1910) put Confucian studies in a new context, developed the native Sil-Hak *(Practical Science), and met the rising influence of Western thought and Christianity. It is no exaggeration to say that the spiritual culture of Korea became a reservoir where various streams of Eastern culture joined.*

The development of classical music in Korea is a good example, channeling the best of musical styles originating in the western Asian regions, the Chinese mainland, Mongolia and Manchuria. Korea suffered considerable cultural loss in war and through the Confucian-oriented cultural policies of Yi rulers. Yet, as history proves, the Korean culture served in many ways as the melting-pot of various Asian cultural traditions.

The 24 Korean Characters

Unlike the Chinese ideograph or the Japanese kana, *characters of the Korean Hangul are phonetic symbols like the alphabet. Hangul consists of 10 vowels and 14 consonants.*

CONSONANTS / **VOWELS**

	ㅏ a	ㅑ ya	ㅓ ŏ	ㅕ yŏ	ㅗ o	ㅛ yo	ㅜ u	ㅠ yu	ㅡ ŭ	ㅣ i
ㄱ K(G)	가 K(G)a	갸 K(G)ya	거 K(G)ŏ	겨 K(G)yŏ	고 K(G)o	교 K(G)yo	구 K(G)u	규 K(G)yu	그 K(G)ŭ	기 K(G)i
ㄴ N	나 Na	냐 Nya	너 Nŏ	녀 Nyŏ	노 No	뇨 Nyo	누 Nu	뉴 Nyu	느 Nŭ	니 Ni
ㄷ T(D)	다 T(D)a	댜 T(D)ya	더 T(D)ŏ	뎌 T(D)yŏ	도 T(D)o	됴 T(D)yo	두 T(D)u	듀 T(D)yu	드 T(D)ŭ	디 T(D)i
ㄹ R(L)	라 R(L)a	랴 R(L)ya	러 R(L)ŏ	려 R(L)yŏ	로 R(L)o	료 R(L)yo	루 R(L)u	류 R(L)yu	르 R(L)ŭ	리 R(L)i
ㅁ M	마 Ma	먀 Mya	머 Mŏ	며 Myŏ	모 Mo	묘 Myo	무 Mu	뮤 Myu	므 Mŭ	미 Mi
ㅂ P(B)	바 P(B)a	뱌 P(B)ya	버 P(B)ŏ	벼 P(B)yŏ	보 P(B)o	뵤 P(B)yo	부 P(B)u	뷰 P(B)yu	브 P(B)ŭ	비 P(B)i
ㅅ S	사 Sa	샤 Sya	서 Sŏ	셔 Syŏ	소 So	쇼 Syo	수 Su	슈 Syu	스 Sŭ	시 Si
ㅇ ng	아 A	야 Ya	어 Ŏ	여 Yŏ	오 O	요 Yo	우 U	유 Yu	으 Ŭ	이 I
ㅈ Ch(J)	자 Ch(J)a	쟈 Ch(J)ya	저 Ch(J)ŏ	져 Ch(J)yŏ	조 Ch(J)o	죠 Ch(J)yo	주 Ch(J)u	쥬 Ch(J)yu	즈 Ch(J)ŭ	지 Ch(J)i
ㅊ Ch'	차 Ch'a	챠 Ch'ya	처 Ch'ŏ	쳐 Ch'yŏ	초 Ch'o	쵸 Ch'yo	추 Ch'u	츄 Ch'yu	츠 Ch'ŭ	치 Ch'i
ㅋ K'	카 K'a	캬 K'ya	커 K'ŏ	켜 K'yŏ	코 K'o	쿄 K'yo	쿠 K'u	큐 K'yu	크 K'ŭ	키 K'i
ㅌ T'	타 T'a	탸 T'ya	터 T'ŏ	텨 T'yŏ	토 T'o	툐 T'yo	투 T'u	튜 T'yu	트 T'ŭ	티 T'i
ㅍ P'	파 P'a	퍄 P'ya	퍼 P'ŏ	펴 P'yŏ	포 P'o	표 P'yo	푸 P'u	퓨 P'yu	프 P'ŭ	피 P'i
ㅎ H	하 Ha	햐 Hya	허 Hŏ	혀 Hyŏ	호 Ho	효 Hyo	후 Hu	휴 Hyu	흐 Hŭ	히 Hi

23

Korea's originality developed through the process of acculturation in many fields, the arts as well as science and technology.

Korea invented the world's first movable metal type for printing in 1234, more than 200 years before Gutenberg's invention of Western type in 1450. Koreans invented a rain-gauge during the reign of King Sejong the Great (1419-50), the fourth king of the Yi dynasty. The Koryo celadon glaze pottery of the 15th and 16th centuries is yet unmatched in its outstanding quality. The world's first iron-clad warships were built by Admiral Yi Sunsin (1545-1598).

Above all, a national alphabet known as Hangul, invented by King Sejong in the 15 century, represents the superb creativity of the Korean people. This alphabet is one of the most outstanding inventions of mankind. Designed in a remarkably scientific system of vowel and consonant notation, it was planned by King Sejong to replace Chinese ideographs, as an aid to popular literacy. It is regarded as the essence of Korean culture.

When we reflect upon the remote past of our long history, we realize that Koreans are truly a self-reliant, democratic people with a highly developed culture and that Korea is, in its historic essence, a peace-loving nation, though it has often been compelled to defend itself against invasions.

The Korean national spirit finds its roots in the ancient founding principle of the nation known as hongik ingan—*or "the welfare of the masses," as well as the knightly ethic of the United Silla period known as* hwarangdo chongsin, *the* hwarang *spirit. The term* hongik ingan, *which may be translated as "give much help to the multitude," was the creed of the mythological Tangun, at the time of his legendary founding of the nation. It implies that both the individual and the state have the obligation to help others, making men in all walks of life brethren in the true sense. This philosophy finds a consistent modern expression in today's peaceful democracy.*

The hwarang-do *was a collective movement of young men in Silla who devoted themselves to the cultivation of knighthood and comradeship based upon a common creed—the knights errant of Korean chivalry. This young elite made inspection tours to provinces, reporting their findings on people's living conditions to the government. They recommended talent, commended merit, and punished injustice.*

In developing personality, the hwarang *movement emphasized the cultivation of benevolence, wisdom, filial piety and loyalty. As a device of early political education, it nourished a spirit of generosity and an awareness of individual as well as social rights. Unlike the Japanese samurai, who overstressed their rigid concept of battle and death, the* hwarang *preferred the combination of the pen and the sword. The ideal personality of those Silla people was partially expressed in the two aspects of the Sokkuram Stone Cave Temple—dignity and grace.*

The rise and decline of dynasties during more than 4,000 years of history provided Koreans with valuable lessons. The nation flourished whenever the

*The underwater mausoleum of King Munmu of the
Silla Dynasty, who died in 681 A.D., located
off the east coast of North Kyongsang Province.
The royal coffin was laid on the peaceful sea bottom,
protected by huge rocks, approximately
200 yards off shore.*

hongik ingan *and* hwarang *spirit prevailed, but it declined whenever these deteriorated. For instance, they flourished when Silla accomplished the unification of the three ancient kingdoms into one state, whereas they were deficient when the Yi dynasty was deprived of its sovereignty by the Japanese.*

The 2,000 years up to the end of the 19th century were a period of defensive resistance against foreign invasions; they also represented a vigorous national creativity. But the most recent 100 years, from the late 19th century to the middle of the 20th, were marked by darkness and suffering.

Korea was not successful in its early attempts at modernization. The Korean people brought to culmination their "national disgrace" by surrendering to the Japanese imperialists on August 29, 1910. And during the 36 years of Japanese rule we were never free from Japanese exploitation.

We had our enlightenment movements initiated by pioneer thinkers, and we often struck out against foreign domination — as in the Samil Independence Movement (March 1, 1919), in which the people fought vainly against armed Japanese gendarmes with their bare fists. Yet our politicians were mostly corrupt and inefficient, and enlightenment movements ended without fruitful results. Nor was the Samil Independence Movement able to restore the nation's sovereignty, due to the absence of favorable conditions within the country and abroad.

We obtained our freedom from foreign rule only

following Japan's surrender to the Allies at the end of World War II.

Yet at the moment of liberation the land was divided and Korea's high hopes were shattered, disappearing completely with the Communist invasion of June 25, 1950.

But for Koreans the ordeal of the 1950's was not a useless one. The harsher our trials become, the more rigorously the nation examined itself as to their causes. Such self-examination gradually awakened the majority of Koreans to the need for seeking after their own self-reliance, independence, prosperity, and peace. The first fruit of this awakening was the April 19, 1960, student revolution, a campaign of national salvation that aimed to eliminate the rule of the Liberal Party, which had become a symbol of corruption and inefficiency in modern Korea. Then came the May 16, 1961, military revolution, a decisive step toward national reconstruction.

Nine years have since elapsed. Now, as we move ahead into the 1970's, our role and our perspective have changed.

After a hundred years of deteriorating domestic politics and brutal foreign invasion, modern Korea has shaken off the memory of past hardships to find a new kind of excellence in its dramatic social and economic reconstruction. For the military revolution of 1961 enabled the country, for the first time, to set itself singlemindedly on the path of concerted recovery.

Today one can look over the rising city of Seoul, amazed to see a forest of new steel and concrete skyscrapers in a city that slumbered through past years as

28

a dusty ex-Japanese colonial capital. With its new enterprises, banks, communications, hotels, industries, and cultural centers, Seoul has become one of the world's metropolises, a city of hope, 5 million strong, nestling below the venerable scarred mountains that have historically guarded it from invasion. In the shadows of new girders and construction cranes nestle the palaces and monuments of former times.

New six-lane highways link Seoul with Pusan in the south and other centers of the country. (It can be said that 63 per cent of Korea's population is now served by the Seoul-Pusan artery.) The new steel and chemical plants in the Ulsan-Pusan and the Seoul-Inchon complexes are symbols of a rising economy, just as the recently founded research center in the Korean Institute of Science and Technology bears witness to Korea's commitment to the future.

The national product itself increased by 222 per cent between 1961, the year of the Military Revolution, and 1969. It is perhaps a more dramatic index of Korea's rise as an economic power to note that exports which totaled a mere $20 million in 1959 rose to fully $700 million in 1969.

We Koreans have a brilliant history and tradition. But we should also interpret the unfortunate aspects of our history as valuable and worthy, for it is the examination of our unfortunate recent past rather than boasts about the glories of our ancient history, that gives a stronger impetus to our self-awakening.

At the threshold of the 1970's, a decade in which

Gilt-bronze standing Buddha:
From Uiryong, Southeastern Korea.
Height 6-3/4 in.
Koguryo Dynasty, A.D. 539?
National Museum of Korea.

*we are determined to attain tremendous goals of na-
tional reconstruction — self-reliance, independence,
prosperity and the eventual unification of our divided
homeland — let us reflect upon the past 100 years of
continued deterioration, confusion, suffering and mis-
ery. Let us evaluate our present and speculate on the
prospects of our future.*

chapter one

trials and awakening

The Stormy Wave of Imperialism

In international politics, power tends to flow from the higher to the lower planes. In the age of imperialism, in particular, several dominant currents flowed toward power vacuums on the globe. A nation situated in a power vacuum is likely to become an arena of competition among powerful nations. Such a power vacuum was responsible for the Korean people's tragedy, in which they lost the national sovereignty they had maintained for over 4,000 years and were driven into a state of subjugation and stagnation.

In the mid-19th century, when Korea still slumbered in national seclusion, her shores were battered by the tides of imperialism, reinforced by the continuous Anglo-Russian rivalry throughout the 19th century.

The occupation of Komun Island (Port Hamilton) by

a British fleet in April, 1885 signaled for the first time the recognition by world powers of the importance of the Korean peninsula. The British occupation, a swift move to counter the secret agreement between Russia and Korea on concessions in Yonghung Bay (Port Lagarett), came to an end two years later with the explanation by the Korean government that the accord was not a formal one.

The Port Hamilton incident might well have marked the decisive moment for Korea to turn her eyes toward the outside world, but the royal court did not sufficiently grasp the meaning of the incident or the warning it contained.

Concurrently with the onslaught of European imperalism, another tidal wave swept across the Korean peninsula. This was the turmoil resulting from the collision of the policies of Ch'ing China and imperial Japan, which had been engaged in a dangerous confrontation over Korea.

It was inevitable that Japan, advancing on the Asian continent after having completed its domestic reorganization, would enter into a bitter contest with China over hegemony in Korea.

Japan, which grasped the essence of international politics in its own development as a modern nation-state, did not oppose the surging tide of imperialism. It allowed the alien tide to flow by rather than engulf it. Indeed, Japan formed a substream in the current of European imperialism, and made its debut on the Korean peninsula under the guise of promoting Korean independence.

Stone head of Buddha: From Kyongju area. Height 15-1/2 in. Great Silla Dynasty, ca. second half of 8th century. National Museum of Korea.

Japan first sought to sever the traditional relationship between the Ch'ing and Korea. The first result of this Korean policy was the Ganghwa Treaty in 1876, which provided that Korea should open its ports to the outside world for the first time.

Ch'ing China also made a persistent effort to retain its suzerainty over Korea, that special arrangement between the two countries which Western scholars term "vassal relations." The confrontation between the Ch'ing and Japan continued for over 10 years with first one side, then the other, gaining the advantage. The two countries began a war for supremacy in the Korean peninsula, ending in a one-sided victory for Japan in 1895 with China expelled from the Korean peninsula. Japan then demanded "special concessions" from the Korean government as compensation. It intervened in Korea's domestic affairs by placing so-called consultants in every agency of the Korean government, by which means the actual power was secured.

However, the real struggle among the imperialist powers was yet to begin. Russia, its European borders secured by its alliance with France, initiated the contest with an advance into Asia. It forced Japan to return to China the Liaotung peninsula, obtained in accordance with the Shimonoseki Treaty (1895) after the Sino-Japanese war. Russia began to challenge Japan's "special privileges" on the Korean peninsula, encouraged by the successful Russian occupation of Manchuria following the Boxer Rebellion.

This Russian intervention caused a series of upheavals in Korean political circles. A Korean queen was killed by a group of Japanese assassins, and the emperor moved to the Russian legation for safety.

On January 30, 1902, Great Britain, abandoning its traditional policy of non-interference, allied itself with Japan and intervened in Korea to check Russia's southward expansion.

U.S. President Theodore Roosevelt criticized the Korean people for not even so much as clenching their fists to promote their own national interests. However, it may well have been that no matter how firmly the Koreans clenched their fists, it was too late for them to save their nation. After the Russo-Japanese war had swept across the Korean peninsula, scarcely a vestige of an independent Korea remained.

We were powerless. What could be found in Korea in the age of imperialism was a power vacuum. Neither the Korean government nor its ruling class possessed the capability of mobilizing the people for the nation's defense. The caste-ridden ruling class curried foreign favor in its own struggles. This served only to aggravate frictions between the world powers involved.

This desperate state of affairs, however, did not extinguish the spirit of self-reliance which the Korean people had demonstrated down through their long history. Not all of the people continued to remain in deep sleep. Amid the shock and confusion of the 20-odd years from the dawn of enlightenment to the loss of national sovereignty, one group of pioneers found lessons in the penetrating knowledge of history and reality it possessed. Retaining the hope of their forefathers, these men strove for a new, bright future.

Kyonghoi-lu, an ancient banquet pavilion
of Kyongbok Palace in Seoul,
is surrounded by a broad and airy veranda
and stands on 48 original monoliths,
each 16 feet high
and almost a yard across.
The present building
dates back only as far as 1867,
although the palace was
founded more than five centuries ago.
The original structure,
save for the granite pillars,
was destroyed in an early war.

Pioneers of Modernization

Long after Western society had realized itself in the Renaissance and the Reformation, and liberated itself from feudalism through the American Revolution, the French Revolution and the Industrial Revolution, Korea remained fast asleep. Only after the two foreign invasions in the middle part of the Yi dynasty era—the Japanese in 1592 and the Manchus in 1636—did our leaders awaken to the need of modernity and modern national defense. Two great scholars lived at that time—Yi Hwang (Toige, 1501-70) and Yi I (Yulgok, 1536-84)—whose Confucian learning surpassed that of their contemporaries. Their thought, however, was highly speculative in nature and aloof from reality.

It was, therefore, the school of Practical Science, *Sil-Hak* that first proposed to augment the metaphysical learnings of Confucianism with research into practical problems. This school, expanding its scope by absorbing knowledge from China and broadening contact with European thought, carried the first torch lit for national modernization. Scholars of the Practical Science school made a strenuous effort to embody their theories in state policy and to utilize them for national projects. But the political situation existing at that time prevented the government from accepting their ideas.

Although Practical Science failed to achieve any great political results, it offered many plans for a better society, including reforms in government, taxation, education and national defense. This spirit was subsequently incorporated in the social reform initiated by Christianity, introduced into Korea from China in the early part of the 19th century.

Confucianism, long the supreme principle of government, had made too rigid a distinction between the aristocrats and the common people, regarded knowledge of the Chinese classics as the ultimate status symbol, and discriminated greatly against women. The principle of equality advocated by the Christian religion, therefore, found ready acceptance among the oppressed commoners and women. The Korean version of the Bible, written entirely in the Hangul alphabet, facilitated the rapid propagation of Christianity, and this religion contributed to the increased awareness of human rights.

Because Christianity contradicted traditional Confucian thought, however, government leaders for a long time severely oppressed Christians. Consequently Christianity, despite the fact that it had made great contributions to social reform in other parts of the world, had little practical effect in Korea.

The modernization drives launched by both Practical Science scholars and Christians failed because feudalistic politicians either opposed or neglected them. Thus the Korean people lost a precious opportunity to reform their society before they were drawn into the whirlpool of imperialist encroachment.

Reform movements up to that time had rejected excesses, advocating only gradual social renovation in the face of oppression. However, as the Korean government, unable to counter the imperialist threat, simply assumed a flattering attitude towards it, Korean pioneers, anxious

Famed throughout Asia,
the mysterious tonic effect
of Korean ginseng for
prolonging the prime of life
is attributed to a divine being within the
unique Korean root herb.
As it is much sought after in
the world market and particularly
in Southeast Asia,
cultivation of Korean ginseng is a
highly specialized type of farming for export.

about national survival, attempted more radical social reform. Two epoch-making incidents dramatized this movement—the Gapsin Political Incident and the Tonghak Revolution.

The Gapsin incident of October 27, 1884, was brought about by the Kaehwa Tongnip party (The Independence Club) led by Kim Okgyun (1851-94), and other progressive young patriots. Unlike the conservative politicians in power, these men correctly grasped the international situation and felt the need for modernization.

They aimed at eradicating the conservative faction depending on China. Drawing a lesson from the experience of Japan, which had achieved rapid development, these progressives were convinced that modernization alone could guarantee national survival.

The 14-point reform policy they put forth made it clear that they intended to bring tributary diplomacy to an end and to restore Korea's national prestige. They demanded that the tyranny of the nobility be eliminated and that the people be guaranteed equal rights. They proposed that in the interests of economy government systems be simplified, asserting at the same time that government discipline should be strictly enforced by eradicating fraudulent practices and punishing corrupt officials. They advocated the establishment of modern police and military systems, proposed a modern political system based on government by consensus, a modern social welfare policy for the poor and amnesty for political offenders. In short, their aim was to organize a modern democratic government based on nationalism and self-reliance.

This great step forward, however, was tragically

frustrated within three days. Aided by Japanese betrayal and Chinese intervention, conservatives were able to crush the young revolutionaries.

If a movement aims to secure abundant living for the masses, then it is necessary that they be awakened to the need for modernization. But only a few pioneers had realized this need, while the thinking of the masses was still governed by premodern consciousness. This being the case, the poorly planned reform movement initiated by Kim Okgyun and his party failed to gain popular support.

Also, although the engineers of the Gapsin Incident needed to watch closely the movements of both China and Japan, they were negligent in that they trusted Japan excessively, and failed to anticipate Chinese intervention.

Ten years after the Gapsin Incident, on March 21, 1894 (the 31st year of King Kojong's reign, 1864-1907), Jeon Bongjun (1854-95) and his followers rose up against the government in Kobu, Chollado Province, in what is known as the Tonghak Revolution. This was an unprecedented spontaneous popular revolt. Whereas the Kaewha Tongnip group sought Western-style modernization, the Tonghak Revolution aspired to modernize on the basis of Oriental thought. The ideological basis for the revolt was the religion called Tonghak (later called Chondo-gyo), among whose tenets was the doctrine that God and man are equal, or rather, that God resides within man.

The religion was named Tonghak (Eastern Learning) to set it in opposition to Christianity, which was then called Sohak (Western Learning). In fact, however, Tonghak adopted much of the Christian doctrine, along with strains of Confucianism, Buddhism and Taoism. Two

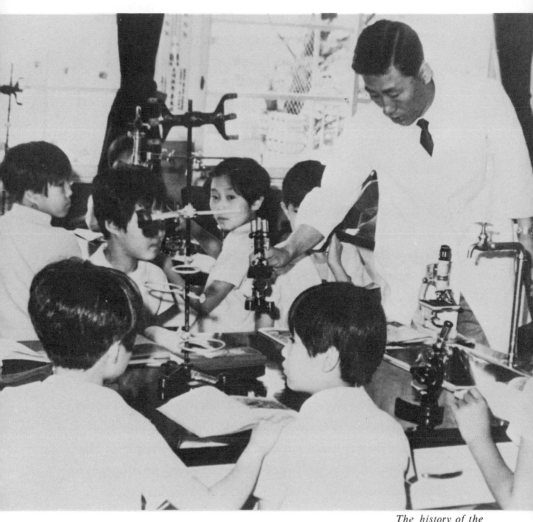

*The history of the
civilization of mankind is
very closely related to the
history of scientific
and technical development.
Korea's efforts to cast off
an underdeveloped economy will
be best accomplished through
the promotion of science and technology,
using the wisdom and talents
of its people as a great resource.*

of its concepts were conspicuous—one a strong national dedication to prevent the nation from being overwhelmed by European powers and Japan, while the other was a populist call for universal equality. This was directed at helping commoners suffering under the tyranny of the nobility.

Tonghak won a large number of converts, especially among farmers, but it was hated by the ruling class and subjected to ruthless persecution as an heretical religion. Its founder was executed. Its believers eventually broke out in rebellion and won considerable, if short-lived, influence on a new spirit of reform throughout the country. But the royal court, to its disgrace, responded with a campaign of subjugation, requesting Chinese assistance which, in turn, invited Japanese intervention. Within a year, the peasants' revolution was over.

The 12-point reform proposal the Tonghak rebels put forth was a far more ardent expression of desire for modernization than the policy which had been pursued by the leaders of the Gapsin Incident. They first called for a purge of corrupt officials and for the punishment of dishonest wealthy people and the Yangban (aristocracy). They advocated liberation of serfs, and their demand for permission for widows to remarry indicates that they planned not only political but also social reform. They demanded the abolition of various taxes and the exemption of poor people from the repayment of loans. They called for land reform. And they tried to maintain the national identity by professing a desire to cooperate with the government, calling for punishment on those who collaborated with the Japanese.

The Tonghak Revolution failed first of all because of poor leadership, a failure to understand the political situation, and an inability to organize and train the masses. The second cause of its failure was the intervention by neighboring imperialist powers. It is sad that the modern awakening of the peasantry was trampled down by China and by the armed intrusion of modernized Japan. Nevertheless, the nationalistic and democratic spirit with which the farmers defied the aggression of neighboring powers, and their zeal for social reform, remained vividly in the minds of the people and provided a strong foundation for subsequent modernization movements.

Although the two reform attempts failed, the conservative government was stimulated to make some changes. A reformist cabinet was appointed with Kim Hongjip (1842-96) as the prime minister. The new cabinet undertook reform of the political, economic, and social systems on a broad scale. The so-called Gabo Kyongjang (Gabo Reform), had as its main features:

1. Establishment of a basis for independence
2. Revision of the royal household law to clarify the succession and the limits of royal kinship
3. Consultation with cabinet ministers by the king; the queen and members of her family should not intervene in affairs of state
4. Separate administration of the royal household
5. Definition of the jurisdiction for each agency of the government
6. Legal system of tax collection
7. Systematized tax collection and government expenditures
8. Economies in the royal household
9. Introduction of a budget system

Natural scenic beauty, ancient cultural relics,
and a very pleasant climate
combine to make Korea abundant in
tourist opportunities.
During the past decade
Korea has upgraded tourist facilities
and added modern ones, such as
Walker Hill Resort on the outskirts of Seoul.
Under a government policy
of earning foreign exchange through
such "invisible trade," many
Western-style accommodations have been built.

46

10. Revision of and limitation of authority of the local government systems
11. Education of able youths abroad
12. Establishment of a modern military system
13. Revision of the civil and criminal codes
14. Appointment of competent persons to government positions regardless of their family lineage.

Korea's modernization really began with the Gabo Reform, which was a direct reflection of the spirit manifested in the Gapsin Incident and the Tonghak Revolution. However, the reform policy was enforced by the coercive force of Japanese troops rather than by the Korean government acting on its own. For this reason the people did not pin their hopes on it, and no substantial results were achieved—except for the employment of Japanese consultants in the Korean government. Since this paved the way for Japan's imperialist aggression, it led the Korean people to view later attempts at modernization with suspicion.

Despite this the Korean pioneers, yearning for the modernization of their country, became ever more convinced that such a movement demanded the voluntary participation of an awakened people. The *Tongnip Hyophoe* (Independence Association) was formed in 1896 under the leadership of Seo Jaepil (1864-1951), who exiled himself to the United States after the Gapsin Incident and returned home later. The association was the first popular nationwide modernization movement without any foreign influence lurking behind it, quite different from both the Gapsin Incident and the Gabo Reform. It was also not a class struggle spearheaded by the lower classes, as was the case in the Tonghak Revolution. This enabled the association to win a following and support among young students. Dr. Seo founded the *Tongnip Shinmun (The Independent),* written entirely in Hangul, in 1896, in the conviction that the masses' cooperation was essential for any successful modernization movement.

Through its editorial columns, Dr. Seo emphasized the defense of national sovereignty through national unity. He asserted the importance of mass education to an independent country, and he launched an enlightenment movement covering all fields of national life, including the improvement of clothing, food, and housing, the elimination of superstitions and superstitious practices, and the betterment of sanitation and hygiene. In the political field, he insisted that the government must discard its reliance on foreign countries, and must put democracy into practice by guaranteeing civil rights. At the same time, he assailed the government and the world powers for the former's impotence and the latter's aggressive moves.

Dr. Seo also launched a large-scale civil rights movement through the *Tongnip Hyophoe.* The Independence Gate was erected to symbolize a stronger self-reliant attitude. At a mass rally on Chongno Avenue, Seoul, on October 29, 1898, Dr. Seo attacked the government for its subservient attitude and adopted a six-point reform proposal, which the Emperor Gojong (1864-1907) was asked to implement immediately. The association in three months expanded its membership to more than 10,000.

Youthful leaders such as Yun Chiho, Yi Sangjae and

*In the mountainous regions
winter is rigorous,
offering opportunities for the
outdoor sports favored by many Koreans.*

49

Syngman Rhee took part in the activities of the Independence Association with impressive zeal. However, there were many obstacles hindering the association's activities. Reactionary forces, now determined to crush the activities of the Independence Association, formed the *Hwangguk Hyophoe* (Imperial Association) to head off reform proposals to the emperor. Thousands of its members gathered to assault the association's mass rally. When the Independence Association expanded its civil rights movement, conservatives resorted to even more oppressive measures: the Independence Association was ordered to disband and its leading figures were arrested. The civil rights movement subsequently began to decline.

It should be remembered that the imperialist powers, Japan, Great Britain and Russia, worked very effectively to insure the emergence of the conservatives as an organized political force to oppose the modernization movement. After the Independence Association disbanded, the pioneers were unable to develop another well-organized movement.

If any of the several reform attempts—those golden opportunities for national modernization—had been successful, we would not have experienced the tragedy and disgrace of losing our sovereignty.

It is needless to point out that an incessant struggle to galvanize our people was fought by our patriots, displaying at home and abroad a defiant energy. Worthy of mention are the Heungsadan Movement led by An Chang Ho (1878-1938) and others, the press activities of Chang Jiyeon (1864-1921) and other journalists, the martyrdom of Min Yeonghwan (1861-1905) and other patriots, the suicide of emissary Yi Jun (1859-1907) at The Hague peace conference, the assassination of Hirobumi Ito by An Jungkeun (1878-1910), the operations of forces for independence in every part of the country, and the efforts of teachers to educate the people to govern themselves.

But the masses, having lived under a tyrannical feudal rule for so long, were more accustomed to resignation than to resistance. The politicians in power were blind to the course of history, and the imperialist powers cleverly utilized the politicians' blindness. Eventually, the Ulsa Treaty was concluded with Japan in 1905, paving the way for Japan's formal annexation of Korea on August 29, 1910. The pioneers of modernization were arrested, imprisoned or driven underground. Some went into exile. However, the seeds these abortive reform movements had sown started to grow. The nation's will to independence intensified.

The Declaration of an Independent People

From 1910 until their liberation in 1945, the Korean people underwent a humiliating trial.

Japanese colonial policy, keynoted by military oppression from start to end, paid no heed to world opinion. It suppressed all antagonistic ideologies and activities, and even attempted to annihilate our national culture. Yet the more harsh the Japanese colonial rule of Korea became, the more firmly did our spirit of self-reliance develop into organized resistance.

Even in the darkness shrouding Korea around 1910, several rays of light could be discerned. The struggle for

*The common people in Korea
have always enjoyed
a thriving tradition of mask plays—
half-pantomime, half-ballet,
featuring earthy satire and horseplay.*

the recovery of the nation's sovereignty now moved outside Korea. Organized in America were the Heungsadan (1913) and the Tongjiwhoe (1914), while the Bumindan (1912) came into being in Manchuria.

After the end of World War I, the Korean independence movement became very animated. Conspicuous among overseas activities in and after 1919 were the Korean Students' Conference on Independence held in Japan, the independence movement in China with the French concession in Shanghai as its center, and the submission of an appeal for Korean independence by an assembly of Korean residents in the United States.

The Korean press was still in its infancy at that time, but it was resolute in denouncing political and social elements which it regarded as detrimental to independence. The birth of a national press in the last years of independent Korea coincided with the downfall of the nation itself. Korean journalists therefore were acutely aware of their mission to reflect the national spirit.

An undercurrent of enlightenment was the ideal of civil rights. It was only natural that nationalistic resistance was first generated by the people's indignation at the loss of their civil rights. The conviction gradually took root that to serve their country was to sacrifice themselves not for a king, as they had believed before, but for the Korean people as a whole. Thus they realized the restoration of the nation did not mean the revival of a dynasty.

The enlightenment, or new culture movement, propagated such concepts. For the only method of resistance for the Koreans after having lost their independence was to launch a new culture movement, which then grew into an independence movement. Herein lies the special nature of the modernization movement undertaken during the Japanese rule. Korean leaders remaining at home engaged mostly in cultural and religious activities after 1910 but, ultimately, became the vanguard of the independence movement.

As the combination of cultural enlightenment and national pride penetrated into the minds of the people, despite the various adverse circumstances under which their leaders had to operate, a large-scale nationwide resistance became possible.

On March 1, 1919, an unprecedented wave of anti-Japanese demonstrations took place in a concerted resistance movement which erupted in every part of the country and gradually spread to embrace all the people.

The scale of the movement can be judged by the following figures: About 1,442 rallies were held mobilizing 2,051,448 persons. Of these, 7,509 were killed and another 46,306 were arrested by the Japanese police. These figures are only estimates. Nonetheless they suggest how extensively people participated in the March 1 independence movement.

The movement was elaborately planned well in advance by patriots in exile and a few leaders at home. A group of 33 leaders of the major religions—Chondo-gyo, represented by Son Byeonghi (1861-1922), Christianity and Buddhism—drew up the "Declaration of Korea Independence" and placed their signatures on it: "We

President Heinrich Luebke (right)
of the Federal Republic of Germany
visited Korea
March 2 through 5, 1967.
He was returning the author's
state visit to his country
on December 6 through 15, 1964,
at which time the
two governments agreed to expand
economic cooperation between
Korea and Germany.

hereby proclaim this to the world and to our posterity, demand our just right of national survival, and appeal to mankind's sense of justice."

The declaration made clear to all the nation's will to independence by reiterating that Japan's annexation of Korea was against universal justice.

The movers of the March 1 uprising were a nationalist elite, who, influenced by Japan and the United States, had developed a modern consciousness and a firm belief in nationalism. But students also played an important role. Woodrow Wilson's Fourteen Points, set down as the basis of a World War I peace settlement, provided the direct impetus for the March 1 movement—most notably, the American President's principle of national self-determination.

Korea was moving with the time. During World War I, liberation movements had broken out among the oppressed peoples in Ireland, Egypt, Turkey, India and China. After the war, many countries in Central and Eastern Europe regained or attained independence through this principle, Czechoslovakia, Poland and Yugoslavia among them.

Whether President Wilson had Korea in mind or not, his doctrine of national self-determination greatly encouraged the Korean people to free themselves. Their leaders moved resolutely because they believed that justice and the trend of world thinking supported them.

Yet how many instances have there been in world history of such an idealistic expression of spirit in the face of tyranny? I recall only the American declaration of 1776. Although 1919, unlike 1776, did not achieve a nation's independence, I am confident that the Korean movement was not inferior in terms of vigor and the loftiness of its ideal. And, notably, the March 1 declaration of independence called for a nonviolent response to tyranny. It emphasized true coexistence, stressing that one should neither be an aggressor nor the victim of aggression. The leaders of the March 1 movement instructed the people only to "demonstrate their free will" and that "even though this is our national demand for justice, humanity, survival and prosperity, we should be careful not to antagonize anyone." While reaffirming a belief in orderly action, they told the people to "demonstrate the nation's just intentions to the last man and to the last minute."

We, the present generation, have many things to learn from our grandfathers, who could confidently express their nationalism even under the political and economic yoke of imperial Japan. It is hoped that foreigners, when evaluating Korea's recent awakening, will not overlook the idealism of 1919 merely because of its lack of immediate results.

As the March 1 movement grew into large-scale nationwide demonstrations of nonviolence, the Japanese tried to suppress it with force. But repression was not so easy; consequently the Japanese government had to change its policy to one of governance through cultural domination. If self-determination had been achieved, Korean-Japanese realtions could have been normalized much earlier and Japan might have avoided its tragic defeat in World War II.

*A Part of an
Ancient Painting:
Portrait of Yi
Hang-bok in an
album leaf, artist
unknown. In ink
and color on paper.
Height 14 in.,
width 19-3/4 in.
Yi Dynasty, 17th
century. Seoul
National University
Museum.*

The principle of national self-determination was likewise embodied in the May 4, 1919 movement in China, and in Gandhi's nonviolent resistance movement in India. Is it an exaggeration to say that the Koreans' awakening to national self-realization for the first time in 1919 became a torch lighting the way for all Asian nationalist movements?

Although the nonviolent demonstrations of March 1 failed to achieve their political objective of restoring independence, they nevertheless renewed world understanding of Korea's situation. They also led directly to the establishment of the "Provisional Government of the Republic of Korea" in Shanghai. This marked a revolutionary turning point in the independence movement. Previously, to Koreans, the independence movement had meant the restoration of the Yi dynasty. Now the sole aim was to be the establishment of a republican form of government. All independence movements, including the armed resistance in Manchuria, were then carried out in the name of the provisional government in Shanghai.

A more valuable result, however, was the people's realization that the only way to achieve independence was to build up their own strength. The colonial policy of Japan, which aimed to exploit Korea to lighten the depression that gripped Japan following World War I, severely impoverished Koreans' lives. Its adverse impact on the rural populace was especially devastating. In order to counter effectively the increased exploitation by Japan, independence movements both at home and abroad gradually resorted to armed resistance.

Journalists grew more active after 1920, receiving

wide support among the people. It was in this period that Koreans for the first time developed full-fledged magazines and private newspapers such as the *Dong-a Ilbo* and the *Chosun Ilbo*. In spite of continuous Japanese interference, these periodicals acted as spokesmen for the nation. It was in the press that the nation's resistance spirit manifested itself as an organized force. The journalists of that time were the symbolic vanguard of the independence struggle, standard-bearers for civil rights, and spokesmen for the people's aspirations.

At the same time, new movements began to bear fruit in various other fields. An effort was made in literature and the arts to produce works on the theme of democratic ideals and to assimilate modern European thought. While expressing discontent and anger at their environment, Korean artists made a continuous effort to search for new modes of expression and a new type of man. The new culture spread to women's and children's movements, and extended to the campaign for a "new mode of life," the encouragement of sports, "the movement to recover the national language" led by the Korean Language Society, and the campaign to increase productivity.

However, such efforts were doomed to frustration as Japan's ambitions became more pronounced. As the Japanese took Manchuria and began their invasion of China, Korea was forced to accept a policy of assimilation aimed at converting the peninsula into a forward military base. The Japanese also conscripted Korean youth, thus denying them an education.

In the 10 years from the middle of the 1930's to liberation in 1945, we were even faced with an attempt to de-

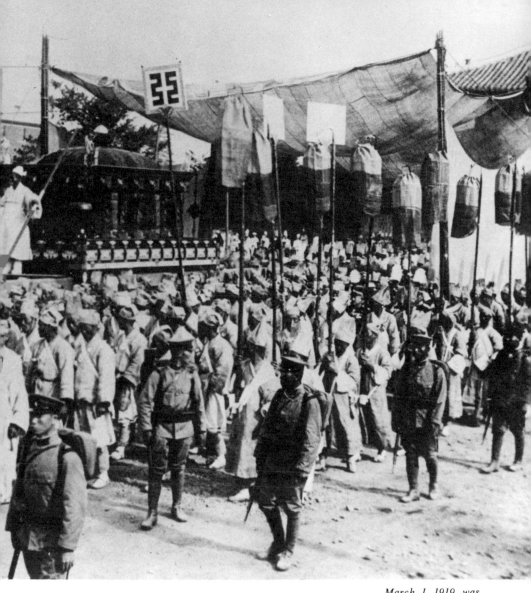

*March 1, 1919, was
the day set for the funeral
of Emperor Kojong, the last monarch
of the Yi Dynasty.
The Korean resistance to Japanese imperialism
seized upon this event
to provide a screen.
Word passed from mouth to mouth
in all the market places
calling for nation-wide demonstrations,
known later as
the Samil Independence Movement.*

61

stroy our language. All efforts directed to modernization disappeared. The national awakening was brought to a halt. "Now the land is lost to others. Does spring come to a stolen field?" This poem aptly describes the painful feelings of a people who had lost their country. They had to wait until the summer of 1945 before spring would come to the fields again.

chapter two

a devout will to find freedom

The Price of Liberation

The joy felt by Koreans on August 15, 1945 is indescribable. Although the liberation from Japan was not achieved by Koreans themselves, the excitement they felt, as a people who had to the last maintained their national pride, was tremendous. The Liberation was a time of justice regained in exchange for years of humiliation and sacrifices.

Contrary to the people's expectations, however, the nation was to experience another period of harsh trials, as if the fates disapproved of its premature joy. Indeed, what awaited was not the glory of independence rebuilt, but tragic division and the menace of Communism.

The division of the nation along the 38th parallel, originally a postwar military arrangement made to speed the surrender of Japanese troops, turned out to be a decisive hindrance to unification. The confrontation between

Taekwon-do,
originally known as Taekyon,
is a Korean martial art
which has been developed through
the last 13 centuries.
Today, it has evolved into not only
a most effective method
of weaponless self-defense,
but also an intricate art,
an exciting sport,
and a trenchant method of
maintaining physical fitness.

64

the U.S. and the U.S.S.R., which jointly occupied Korea, sacrificed Korea's interests to the cold war.

Immediately after Japan accepted the Potsdam Declaration, the Japanese governor-general in Korea selected such prominent Korean figures as Yeo Wunheong, An Jaehong and Song Jinwu to take over authority and maintain public safety. These men soon contacted other associates and organized a Preparatory Committee for Nation-Building.

The Preparatory Committee was not at all content to function as a mere arm of the Japanese administration. It quickly expanded, set up a Students Corps and a Public Safety Corps, and established a foundation for taking over the reins of government.

The Committee, the only political body in the nation at that time, was a mixture of various resistance forces—conservatives and reformists, leftists and rightists, moderates and radicals. It had managed to assemble, though not cohesively, representatives of various sectors of society, including intellectuals and students. The postwar history of Korea might well have been much different had those political leaders shown a positive capacity to take over power. The Preparatory Committee, however, eventually collapsed because its members were involved in internal strife, intensified by the implications of the country's division along the 38th parallel.

Meanwhile, U.S. troops, whose arrival the entire nation had awaited so expectantly, belatedly landed in Inchon on September 8 and went to Seoul the next day. The Japanese national flag, which had flown over Korea for 35 years, was lowered for good that afternoon. Lt. Gen. John

R. Hodge, commanding the U.S. 24th Army Corps, and Adm. Thomas C. Kinkaid, Commander of the U.S. Seventh Fleet, accepted the surrender of Japanese forces south of the 38th parallel.

The U.S. Army, lacking concrete plans for Korean administration, prescribed in the surrender documents that Japanese civil and military officers would continue to perform their normal duties, unless dismissed by the commanding general of the Allied forces.

General Hodge, who finally reached the decision to set up a military government, was later learned to have considered the idea of extending the rule of the Japanese governor-general. Although this idea could not be put into practice due to pressure from Gen. Douglas MacArthur, who had read the minds of the Korean people correctly, General Hodge still chose to retain the existing Japanese administrative network.

Unprepared themselves, the Korean people and their leaders were unable to take any steps against these unpopular measures of the U.S. military government. In addition, the unity of the Preparatory Committee began to weaken, and frustrated conservatives and moderates gradually left it. As leaders who had first rallied around the committee began to abandon it, political groups and factions began to multiply, with the confrontation between radicals and conservatives growing ever more fierce.

Extreme social unrest arose for the want of a stable political force. The disorderly policy of withdrawal adopted by the Japanese governor-general, the inflation

Buddhism reached Korea as early as A.D. 372, and greatly influenced Korean life for the next thousand years. In 1392 it began to decline gradually. Built in 1624, the quintuple-roofed Palsang-jon of Popju Temple in North Chungchong Province today faces a giant modern Buddha made of concrete.

67

born of the excessive issuance of paper money, the market confusion resulting from the theft of stored goods, the paralysis of administrative functions due to the departure of experienced personnel, and the destruction or suspension of operations at production plants formerly operated by the Japanese, all contributed to the chaos. A sense of frustration caused by Korea's artificial division made the situation even worse.

By contrast, the Soviet occupation in North Korea quickly handled the problems related to Japanese surrender, took over administrative power and immediately set up a military government. Upon arrival, the Russian Army soon launched a movement to enlist the support of native nationalists in order to fill the social and political vacuum.

There existed no real Communist foundation in North Korea at the time, and those few Communists released from prisons after the liberation had not received proper Communist training. Most of those who labeled themselves Communists were in fact radical nationalists. The Russian occupation authorities therefore decided that it was still too early for them to carry out a socialist revolution with a Communist force as its core. As a provisional measure, they attempted to mobilize conservative nationalist forces and to combine leftists and rightists to take over power from the Japanese. The full-fledged socialist revolution was to be carried out later, once its organizational basis was established.

By the middle of November, 1945, dual ruling systems had been established in each of the five northern provinces: a Communist Party chapter and a government administration. The Russian occupation forces soon appointed Kim Il-sung, a former Soviet Army captain, as the Communist Party chief and, the following February, Chairman of the North Korean People's Committee, thus completing the initial work for the eventual emergence of a Stalinist-type government in North Korea.

People in the South, disillusioned by political confusion and division, saw a dim ray of hope in the expected return of Dr. Syngman Rhee and other leaders of the Korean provisional government-in-exile. Fifteen key members of the provisional government, including the venerable Kim Koo (1876-1949), returned home to an enthusiastic welcome from the people. Contrary to public expectation, however, the U.S. military government made it clear that these leaders had returned home in an "individual capacity." This attitude reflected the basic U.S. policy of not recognizing the provisional government as legitimate. It may also be that the U.S. military government still hoped to form a single, authentic political force throughout South and North Korea.

As, contrary to U.S. expectations, the 38th parallel division gradually came to be permanent, General Hodge proposed to the commander of the Soviet occupation forces in Pyongyang, Lt. Gen. I. M. Chistiakov, that a political conference be held in Seoul. General Chistiakov refused to accept the offer on the ground that "the unification problem is a matter that should be solved by the U.S. and the Soviet governments."

As World War II
came to an end in 1945,
Korea was liberated
from the Japanese.
The leaders of the
Korean provisional government-
in-exile returned home to
an enthusiastic welcome
from the people.
Contrary to public expectation,
however, the U.S.
military government made it clear
that these leaders
had returned home in
an "individual capacity."

70

Now worried about the existence of the dividing line, the U.S. was compelled to take measures to solve the problem. At the Moscow foreign ministers' conference held in December, 1945, a five-year trusteeship plan for Korea was proposed by U.S. Secretary of State James E. Byrnes, and generally approved. Agreement was reached on four important matters including the establishment of a U.S.-U.S.S.R. Joint Commission for the eventual founding of a provisional government for Korea, as proposed by Soviet Foreign Secretary Molotov.

As soon as the U.S.-Russian trusteeship agreement became known, the Korean people expressed their opposition en masse. On December 31, 1945, endless columns of demonstrators, left and right alike, took to the streets in protest—an intense expression of national indignation by a people firmly determined to regain their sovereignty.

Surprisingly, the Communists and their followers suddenly faced about to support the Moscow agreement. The "Central People's Committee" in North Korea, calculating its political benefits, sent a message of gratitude for the trusteeship agreement. From this time on, the pros and cons of trusteeship became not only a political issue but also a decisive factor accelerating Korea's ideological split.

The U.S.-U.S.S.R. Joint Commission, which met in 1946 and again in March 1947, got nowhere. While the U.S. delegation stressed "freedom of expression," the Russians insisted obstinately on the "eradication of all reactionary elements." While the U.S. side contended that political organizations opposed to trusteeship should also be consulted by the Joint Commission, the Russians insisted that only those parties which supported trusteeship, *i.e.,* only the leftists of the so-called "People's Front," could be consulted.

The Soviet stand clearly revealed Moscow's plans for Korea. It was confirmed by the Soviet delegate who emphasized that "Korea can never be used as a base for an attack on the Soviet Union, but should become a country close and friendly to the Soviet Union."

After the U.S.-U.S.S.R. Joint Commission had virtually broken down, Acting U.S. Secretary of State Robert A. Lovett proposed in a memorandum sent to Soviet Foreign Secretary Molotov that a unified government be established in Korea through general elections, in proportion to population, held throughout South and North Korea under UN supervision. The Soviet Union refused to agree.

When Secretary of State Marshall brought the Korean question to the United Nations, Soviet delegate Andrei Gromyko, erroneously interpreting Article 107 of the UN Charter, opposed the U.S. move. He held it was "illegal to refer a problem resulting from the war, on the solution of which the big powers had already reached an agreement, to the General Assembly."

After the Korean issue was voted a subject for discussion, the Soviet Union, early in 1948, began to propagandize in favor of a simultaneous U.S. and Soviet troop withdrawal from Korea. The Soviet proposal might have seemed to be based on the principle of national self-determination to anyone not familiar with the situation in North Korea at that time. In reality, the Soviet Union had already established the regime headed by Kim Il-sung in the North. Therefore, the Soviet proposal was aimed at capitalizing on what would be a power vacuum in South

Whenever opportunities arise on numerous fact-finding trips around the country, the author enjoys informal chatting with farmers—at times, sharing lunch with them in their fields.

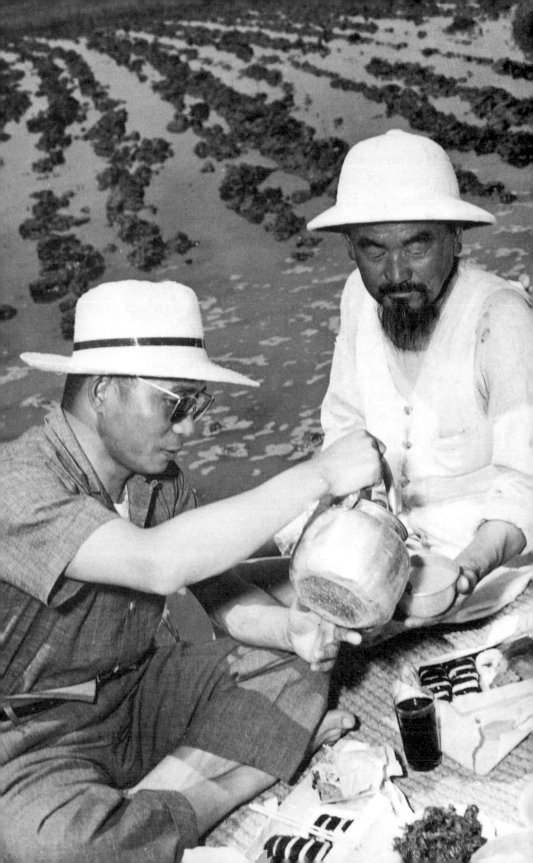

Korea following the withdrawal of U.S. troops, enabling it to take over the South without striking a blow.

When the U.S. delegate proposed to the General Assembly a resolution for free elections throughout Korea, under UN supervision, "to be held by the end of March 1948," the Soviet delegate suggested instead that "representatives of both South and North Korea be invited to the debate on the Korean question," and that "both the U.S. and Soviet troops be withdrawn simultaneously from Korea."

As it was not clear how to determine the qualifications of such representatives from South and North Korea, the U.S. delegation subsequently submitted an amendment resolution proposing that "Korean delegates duly elected be invited to the discussion of the Korean question," and that a United Nations Temporary Commission on Korea be established for the purpose of supervising the elections of those delegates. This amendment resolution submitted by the United States was approved by the UN General Assembly, overriding the original Russian proposal.

Thus, over fierce Russian objections, the Korean question was accepted by the UN. For a while, a general election for the reunification of Korea was in sight. The UN Temporary Commission on Korea commenced its activities early in 1948. But because Soviet opposition made it impossible to hold an election throughout South and North Korea, the committee decided to have one only where this was feasible.

The Soviet Union refused to cooperate with the United Nations, well aware that the Communist organization in North Korea, under the protection of the Soviet military government, would collapse if general elections were held in accordance with the UN resolution. In the face of this intransigence, the first general election ever to be held in Korea was carried out smoothly on May 10, 1948. As had been expected, it resulted in a sweeping victory for the forces supporting Dr. Rhee.

Some Korean leaders were rather cool to the election, feeling it was premature to hold a general election only in South Korea. Yet the election was conducted in a democratic way under the supervision of the UN Temporary Commission, and the voters' turnout officially amounted to 95.5 per cent of the eligible voters—an eloquent expression of a people's will for early establishment of a sovereign government in any form.

The new National Assembly elected Syngman Rhee as speaker and proclaimed the Constitution of the Republic of Korea. The Constitution declared the Korean peninsula and its adjoining islets to be the territory of the republic. This Assembly then elected Rhee President of the country, completing the historical task of founding the government by August 15.

At the same time, the Soviet-backed "People's Committee" in the North proclaimed a constitution and carried out an election of representatives to the People's Council, with the voters voting only "Yes" or "No" on a single and unopposed candidate in each constituency. On September 7, 1948, the Democratic People's Republic of Korea came into being with Kim Il-sung as its chief.

The third UN General Assembly examined a report

During the first Five-Year
Economic Development Plan,
(1962-66), the Government gave heavy stress
to the development
of industrial railroad transportation
linking coal mining areas
on the east coast with
other industrial districts
across the nation.
The second five-year period
envisaged further expansion
of railroad networks and
production of rolling stock.

submitted by the UN Temporary Commission, which re-commended that delegates of the Republic of Korea be invited to the debate on the Korean question before the assembly's Political Committee. It subsequently adopted a resolution which confirmed the existence of the Republic of Korea's only lawful government and recommended that "the occupying powers should withdraw their occu-pation forces from Korea as early as practicable." Follow-ing adoption of the resolution, the United States offered the Republic of Korea *de jure* recognition as of January 1, 1949, and a total of 37 countries followed suit.

Even before the UN General Assembly completed its study of the Korean question, the U.S. began to pull out its troops. President Rhee appealed this action, saying that "any U.S. troop withdrawal before the completion of preparations on the part of Korea to counter a threat of Communist invasion would invite an irreparable misfor-tune for Korea."

The U.S. response to his appeal was rather cool, and the withdrawal of troops was carried out on schedule. By the end of June, 1949, only a small military advisory group of about 500 men remained in Korea. The only assistance that the United States provided was to transfer light wea-pons worth $110 million to the Republic of Korea's new and inexperienced armed forces.

The Republic of Korea's leaders were at a loss what to do. Depending simply on the UN resolution regarding the unification of Korea, few had the farsightedness to realize the imminent danger confronting them. Nor did they demonstrate a high enough level of statesmanship in countering the oncoming danger. While the people were intoxicated by the Republic's establishment and recognition, actually they faced calamity.

The Triumph of Conviction

Preparations for a full-scale invasion southward began in North Korea after establishment of the regime led by Kim Il-sung. Early in 1949, Kim Il-sung himself led a North Korean delegation to Moscow. While in the Soviet capital, he succeeded in concluding a secret agreement with the Soviet Union, in which he was assured additional equipment to outfit six infantry divisions, three cavalry divisions and 150 planes, including 100 fighters.

Through the good offices of the Soviet Union, North Korea concluded a mutual defense treaty with Communist China, and reached an agreement with Peking on transferring the "detachment of Korean troops" stationed in Manchuria and mainland China back to North Korean rule. A number of Korean soldiers serving in the Chinese Communist Army had been returned to North Korea by the end of March, 1950.

By this time, the North Korean regime already had assembled a 200,000-man combat force with a tank division and an armored corps. This constituted the main military force to be used in the invasion of South Korea.

On June 7, the "Extended Central Committee of the Democratic Front for National Unification" adopted an "Appeal for Peaceful Unification," proposing that a general election be held sometime between August 5 and 8 to set up a supreme legislative organization for reunification, that a session of the body thus elected be held in Seoul on August 15, and that a council of representatives of all political parties and social organizations throughout South and North Korea be convened from June 15 through 17, either in Haeju or Kaesong along the 38th parallel. This Communist "peace offensive" was a piece of deception.

At dawn, June 25, 1950, the North Korean Army, supported both by the U.S.S.R. and Red China, launched an all-out attack on the South along all sectors of the 38th parallel with decisively overpowering military strength. The poorly-armed forces of the Republic of Korea encountered an invading enemy equipped with heavy weapons and tanks. One by one, the defense lines fell into the hands of the invaders. The ROK forces retreated southward, like men in a tiny boat confronted by a typhoon.

Fortunately, however, the Korean conflict was quickly brought to the attention of the UN Security Council, thanks to the resolute judgment of President Harry S Truman of the United States. The Security Council approved without delay a set of resolutions calling on the aggressors to stop their act of war, and at the same time recommended that UN member nations render positive assistance to the Republic of Korea to halt the aggression. It also approved the establishment of a UN police force led by the United States. (At the time, the Soviet Union was boycotting the council's sessions.)

President Truman ordered Gen. Douglas MacArthur to dispatch U.S. forces to check the invasion. Subsequently, 16 member countries sent combat troops to Korea pursuant to the UN resolution.

Because of the strong offensive of the Communist forces, the UN and ROK forces in the early stage of the war had to retreat within a defense perimeter based on Pusan. Early in September, however, they launched an all-out counteroffensive. The capital city of Seoul was recaptured after a successful landing of the UN forces in Inchon and the consequent collapse of the Communist invasion force.

Following the crossing of the 38th parallel by the ROK armed forces, the UN troops also began to march north in accordance with the UN resolution on Korean reunification. It seemed as if the people's cherished dream of national reunification would soon become a reality.

But at this point Soviet Premier Josef Stalin, who was anxiously observing the situation in the Korean peninsula, dispatched a special emissary to Mao Tse-tung promising to supply weapons if the Chinese Communists would send reinforcements to Korea. In the beginning of September, the North Korean regime sent a mission to Peking asking for military assistance.

The U.S. Joint Chiefs of Staff at this time sent a directive to General MacArthur telling him to advance to the North provided that the Soviet Union or Communist China would not intervene. Thus it is likely that the United States did not intend to have a military showdown with Russia and Communist China over Korea.

Astutely sensing an extraordinary move by the Communists, President Truman met with General MacArthur on Wake Island and asked him about the possibility of Communist China intervening in the situation. MacArthur confidently assured the President that Peking would not intervene. Quite to the contrary, however, Communist

After the general elections,
the Republic of Korea,
with Dr. Syngman Rhee (right)
as its first President,
was officially inaugurated on the
third anniversary of
the Liberation, August 15, 1948.
The ceremony was attended
by friends from abroad,
including Gen. Douglas MacArthur (center),
then Supreme Commander
of Allied Forces in the Pacific,
and Lt. Gen. John R. Hodge (left),
then Commanding General
of U.S. XXIV Corps.

China had already moved a large number of troops into North Korea.

The UN forces, which had advanced in some places as far as the Yalu and Tumen rivers on the North Korean border, had to fall back due to the mass intrusion of Communist Chinese forces. Although the United Nations branded Red China as an aggressor, the Korean War gradually fell into a stalemate following the dismissal of General MacArthur, who had advocated such punitive measures against mainland China as the bombing of Manchuria and a sea blockade.

While the tide of battle ebbed and flowed, armistice talks were about to take place at the behest of Jakob Malik of the Soviet Union in June 1951. The problem of the disposition of the Korean War became a political issue in the United States, where a presidential election was about to be held. To the people of Korea, it seemed that the U.S. government was making a rather hasty move, prior to the upcoming election, in negotiating for an early armistice even at the sacrifice of the military and political advantages it had obtained in the Korean War. The Korean people, who feared that with an armistice they would lose once and for all this ideal opportunity of reunifying their fatherland by driving the Communist aggressors out of the Korean peninsula, rose up in opposition to the shortsighted truce negotiations the United States began conducting with the enemy.

In these circumstances, President Syngman Rhee suddenly freed all anti-Communist prisoners of war who had been held in numerous POW camps throughout the country. At this time, the truce negotiations were almost in the final stage, and the abrupt release of the anti-Communist POWs unilaterally by the Korean government was a shocking blow to the United States, because the prisoners had been detained under the jurisdiction of the UN forces.

Deeply annoyed, President Dwight D. Eisenhower called Korean Ambassador Dr. Yang Youchan into his office and assailed the Korean government for its action, asking him, "What would you do if the U.S. forces withdrew from Korea?" Ambassador Yang is said to have replied to the angry U.S. President "We would all die!"

The United States could only try to calm the Korean government with friendly persuasion. After lengthy negotiations, Korea and the United States reached an agreement. Korea undertook not to oppose a truce. In return a Korea-U.S. mutual defense treaty would be concluded, 20 ROK Army divisions would be equipped and strengthened with U.S. assistance, and U.S. economic aid for the postwar rehabilitation of Korea would be guaranteed.

The Korean War was a hardship unprecedented even in the history of Korea. During the war, which lasted more than three years, the ROK and U.S. forces suffered 212,000 and 75,000 casualties, respectively, while the loss of human life on the part of the Communist enemy totaled more than 1,190,000. Some 700,000 civilians, too, were either killed or listed as missing. The total number of war victims throughout the country exceeded 3,620,000. The other 15 countries fighting under the UN flag also suffered heavy casualties, while more than 20 other countries gave material and moral support.

In overcoming the hardships of this war, we learned

The two Five-Year Development Plans
included a program for rearrangement
of helter-skelter patches of rice paddies
into more economical patterns
so that modern techniques and mechanical
devices could be used.

at first hand once again how precious freedom is, and we felt the pride of a people increasingly identified with the world community. Throughout the time from the liberation to the Korean War, our people, if they made mistakes, nonetheless proved their ability to survive repeated ordeals. They managed to hold to right reason both through the political confusion preceding 1950 and the fires of war in the 1950's. It must be admitted that the enormous task of later filling the vacuum of the 1950's was a little too heavy for them to bear. But their patience and gallantry facing the challenge of a uniquely horrible war proved to be precious capital for the construction of a stronger Korea.

Communist elements have plotted constantly to overthrow the Republic of Korea by subversion and by the instigation of social unrest. Their well-organized schemes have failed because, once their plots became clear, the masses of innocent people put up stiff resistance. The people's will to freedom has become stronger as time passed, despite the long history of foreign threats to their geopolitically fragile country. This national will was the prime factor in helping us survive our harshest trial.

Throughout this fratricidal tragedy, the Koreans felt to the bone the merciless nature of Communism. This one single experience has contributed much more than any amount of theoretical persuasion toward making Korea the staunchest anti-Communist nation. The Korean people have come to know clearly who their enemy is and what he is like. They have most unmistakably realized the emptiness of what is called "peaceful coexistence."

With the nation still divided, the Korean War, which ended in an armistice, brought neither victory nor defeat. It left not only the remnants and devastation of war, but also a people armed with new determination and an insight that freedom and peace can be enjoyed only by those who can and will fight for them, and that only those peoples who learn something from confusion and trial and continue to advance can be assured of a bright future.

The aftermath of the Korean War was grave, but by no means fatal. Korea gained through the strong ties of mutual cooperation with friendly countries. Yet, because of the war's destruction, the nation had to endure poverty and hunger for several years. Stupefied by the miserable conditions of cities and farming villages which had been reduced to bleak ruins, Korea could not help but rely on the assistance of friendly countries. The links of friendship thus forged in the war were firm and enduring, and the hand of help extended by Korea's allies was a prime source of strength.

Just as every Korean has bitter memories of the Korean War, so do the families of those young warriors from friendly nations who were buried in this land. The memories of this terrible experience should lead us to resolve never to repeat past mistakes. In order to apply the war's lessons to the realities of today, the nation must exert itself to prevent the recurrence of Communist provocations which have recently been increasing both in quantity and intensity. By cultivating our strength and thus warning the enemy against resorting to any foolish action, we can best

Integrated into
the current development plan
is a 20-year
housing construction program
which will enable
every household to own
at least one home.
Efforts are made to
seek construction of more
economical and durable
houses through research,
standardization of materials,
improvement of construction
methods, etc.

recompense the souls of those who died for the sake of freedom.

The stagnancy that prevailed after liberation, and the destruction of the Korean War, caused the nation to lose at least 20 years in its development effort. The national foundation, already weak, was shattered completely by the war. Together with the later confusion and inflation of the war, the land reform of 1948 brought about the downfall of the landowners who had represented the traditional community. Worse yet, the existing strata of organized society underwent drastic change, as millions of uprooted refugees continued to drift about in search of a livelihood.

In such circumstances both government and people resembled sufferers from malnutrition, whose physical condition would not permit them to perform as they wished.

Frankly speaking, the nation existed entirely on the foreign aid granted us for postwar rehabilitation. What else could be done? Nothing but to prepare for the days to come. In anticipation of better days, Koreans made it their major task to promote and improve education—the best way any people can develop their inherent potential.

It is to our credit that we lavished keen attention and unique enthusiasm on the development of education, whether or not we recognized its long range value for our modernization. Since the 17th-century enlightenment period, when our advanced thinkers launched new cultural campaigns under the slogan, "Knowledge is power," education in Korea has been linked closely to a "save-the-nation" movement. Our people have never lost the image of education as the key to the future.

After the war's end, especially, enthusiasm for education began to grow even more intense, due to the people's wartime realization of democracy and the need to be self-reliant. Colleges and middle schools sprouted like mushrooms after a rain. The rate of educational expansion exceeded that of economic expansion many times, to the point where the balance between educational and economic growth could hardly be maintained.

Yet the rebuilding of schools, most of which were destroyed during the war, was a difficult task, and other educational facilities had to be expanded with equal speed. Had the people given up hope for the next generation after the wartime trials of their own, they would have faced a truly bleak future.

Precedents in other countries indicate that economic development should be achieved along with an equally efficient educational development, if a developing country is to achieve early modernization. Korea could hardly have expected the rapid advancement actually attained in the 1960's had it not made such a strenuous effort in the 1950's for the improvement of education.

The Long, Thorny Way to Freedom

President Rhee's Liberal Party government made repeated mistakes in the disposition of postwar problems, which contrasted to its effective and praiseworthy conduct of the war. Its leaders failed to set a real reconstruction in motion despite the obvious economic and moral necessity of such an effort.

Skiing has become
a popular winter sport,
next to ice-skating,
although there are
only a few skiing grounds
in the entire
southern region of
the Korean Peninsula.

The postwar rehabilitation of Korea was carried out mainly through U.S. aid provided by the Mutual Security Act. By the end of 1957 or 1958, the groundwork was almost completed. Accordingly, U.S. aid, which amounted at its peak in 1957 to $554,000,000, started to decrease year by year. Furthermore, U.S. assistance for investment in production facilities was shifted to Development Loan Funds (DLF) in 1958, thus causing a major setback to the economy, which had been increasingly dependent on foreign aid since the war.

Even before the shifting of the U.S. aid to DLF loans, Foreign Operations Administration (FOA) and International Cooperation Agency (ICA) aid was utilized mainly for the procurement of consumer goods and raw materials. Thus, the actual import of production facilities which Korea urgently needed was between $75,000,000 and $95,000,000 annually during the period 1954-1957. It decreased to an all-time low of $30,000,000 in 1958. Large quantities of surplus agricultural products were imported, in the form of aid in accordance with U.S. Public Law 480, (1953), but the money from the sale of aid grain was allocated mainly to national defense expenditures.

As U.S. policy underwent major changes following the new emphasis on peaceful coexistence with Russia, Korea, which had prepared no independent economic foundation, was compelled to bear the enormous expense of building a self-supporting economy. The problem recalled a man trying to cultivate farmland with his bare hands. The government, nevertheless, continued its desperate attempts to obtain more aid from foreign countries—completely overlooking the changing trends in world affairs.

Little successful effort was made to make wise use of this aid, or to actuate an effective policy aimed at making self-reliant economic development possible. Yet, the available labor force expanded day by day, because of rapid population growth. The number of new college graduates also continued to increase. The economy of those days could not support enough industry to absorb all these young people. And the steady increase in the number of well-educated unemployed worsened social unrest and dissatisfaction among the nation's youth.

Concurrently, a small group of tycoons began to monopolize the booming postwar rehabilitation work. These newly rich, in connivance with government officials, neglected both public welfare and private business morals.

A sort of nihilism grew from the horrible experience of war. The extravagent greed for material gains, stimulated by the influx of foreign aid goods, turned the people of Korea in the wrong direction. Social discipline, as well as traditional ethical and moral standards, deteriorated. Yet people were eagerly seeking a national leader and a political force capable of handling state affairs in an impartial manner. The people were impatiently waiting for the "dawn of the nation," when their will and potential, forged in the midst of trial, could be transformed into a driving force for national development.

The brilliant activities of intellectuals during this period were indeed worthy of admiration. Journalists, especially, played an extraordinarily important role with a

Naju Urea Fertilizer Plant:
Five fertilizer plants have been
built since 1961,
producing more than
one million tons of urea
and other
chemical fertilizers each year.
Until mid-1960,
the nation had to import
more than $50 million
of fertilizer annually.
Today Korea is
self-sufficient in fertilizer
and exports
surplus output to
international markets.

sense of mission similar to that shown by the nation's patriotic leaders during the period of Japanese domination. They infused a popular sense of resistance against the incumbent government, bravely exposed all sorts of injustices and roundly criticized governmental corruption.

Young students, well aware of democracy's implications, were also ready to devote their courage to the sublime task of establishing national justice. They had learned historical lessons from various nationwide demonstration movements their seniors had staged against Japan at the sacrifice of their own lives.

The illegal elections held on March 15, 1960, ignited the spirit of patriotism in those students' hearts. On that election day, they staged a street demonstration in Masan, a southern port city, protesting against the illegal conduct of the election. Police fired on them, killing and wounding many of the demonstrators. On April 19, students in Seoul and throughout the country rose up to clamor for democracy and against the Liberal Party government. When demonstrators swarmed into the official residence of the President, police opened fire, killing and seriously wounding a large number of students. Still again on April 25, a group of college professors staged a street demonstration in Seoul. The huge waves of students and citizens who joined those professors filled up main streets and alleys. Soldiers who were rushed to the scene under martial law were obviously sympathetic with the students and people.

President Syngman Rhee was finally compelled to resign his office, bringing to an unhappy end more than 60 years of devotion to the cause of Korean modernization. His efforts in this cause had begun in the closing years of the 19th century when he was a youthful member of the Independence Association. After the loss of Korean independence he had fled abroad to lead the fight for its restoration. In 1919 he was elected president of the provisional government in Shanghai. He had returned to Korea following the liberation from Japanese rule, to become the leader of anti-Communist political forces in the South. In 1948 Rhee was elected first president of the Republic of Korea and was widely hailed as "father of his country" for his efforts to establish a modern democracy and for his successful conduct of the Korean War.

In the latter days of his government, however, misled by assistants concerned with the extension of their own power, he failed to keep contact with the people and lost his awareness of their needs and desires. This failure led directly to the April 19 student uprising and to the unhappy end to Syngman Rhee's distinguished career.

The uprising was a spontaneous movement launched by the people to overcome the political crisis then prevailing, a genuine expression of the love of justice by the students at the risk of their lives. The April 19 uprising, indeed, was a significant civil rights movement aimed at creating a more realistic political climate in which the rights of the people would be guaranteed and the solution to the problems of their living conditions would be dealt with.

Following the April uprising, the Second Republic came into being and the Democratic Party regime led by Chang Myon (John M. Chang) was established. The Chang government came to power by virtue of the April uprising, not through any effort by the Democratic Party. As it turned out, the government was weak and inefficient, not capable of normalizing the social order or of controlling the street demonstrations which became rampant after the April uprising. The nation was driven, accordingly, into an even more chaotic state, nearly beyond control. To make the situation worse, a pro-Communist political force, taking advantage of the confusion, gradually came to the fore. In the spring of 1961, a number of naive students, unconsciously dancing to the tune of these Communist instigators, rashly advocated the opening of unconditional negotiations between South and North Korea at Panmunjom.

The gathering political instability made many people seriously concerned for the country's future. Knowing well our demonstrative spirit of nationalism, they must have foreseen that a revolution in one form or another would take place, in the tradition of the great popular uprisings. All the people, including myself, felt that if the popular will remained dormant, and the situation worsened, this country would eventually become Communist. The 4,000 year old history and tradition of the country would then have come to an end. We would not have the courage to meet the souls of our forefathers, who had struggled hard so that we and our descendants could live in peace and prosperity through the achievement of a national revival.

When my thoughts reached this point, I was overwhelmed with sorrow that I had been born in this land at such a time. I stayed awake nights, planning how I might save the nation from its crisis, by whatever means were available to me. I was a soldier, and I was disinclined to see soldiers get involved in politics. Nevertheless, there is a point beyond which one cannot simply be an onlooker. With the nation on the verge of ruin, with the national economy worsening and the social order deteriorating, my conscience would not allow me to remain concerned with the duty of national defense only. This was, after all, the nation that our soldiers had defended with their lives.

My desire to save the nation from crisis had begun to grow at the end of the Liberal Party, long before the April 19 uprising. The first concrete plan for the military revolution had been drawn up sometime around the March 15 elections. Because of the April 19 uprising, however, our plan was not implemented.

We took it as rather fortunate that a revolution, aimed at the same goal we had, had been achieved by the students and the public rather than by the military. We also hoped that after the April uprising both the political climate and society would be purified. But the national crisis went from bad to worse.

Finally, on May 16, 1961, my comrades and I staged a military revolution. "The military have risen up", we said, "for the purpose of saving the nation which is wandering on the brink of total collapse, in the belief that the fate of our country and people cannot be left any longer in the hands of the corrupt government and politicians."

We also made our future course of action clear and expressed it explicitly in our revolutionary pledges: to strengthen our anti-Communist postures; to eradicate all

President John F. Kennedy
receives the author
at the White House,
on November 14, 1961,
when the latter made his
first state visit to
the United States
to discuss current issues
of mutual interest
between the two allied nations.

corruption; to establish close ties with friendly countries; to build a strong and prosperous country, concentrating our efforts on achieving a self-reliant national economy; and to eventually achieve the territorial reunification long cherished by all our people.

Our prayer for national unification will never be realized with slogans or sentimental theories. The "Let us march north" slogan, prevalent during the days of Liberal Party government, was an imprudent one, which only deepened a tension detrimental to unification. The idea of holding South-North negotiations so loudly proclaimed on the eve of the May 16 revolution was nothing but a naive, sentimental plan.

In order to achieve an early unification, the international situation would have to be favorable. Equally important, we had first to modernize our country, thus strengthening our capability to deal with unification. The only way to win a victory over the Communists is to demonstrate power sufficient to surpass them in the economic, political, social, and all other sectors of life. Sharing this devout belief, I and my comrades of the revolutionary government resolved to toil harder under the pledge, "Unification through victory over Communism."

Our nation's will to national modernization, which had grown steadily during the past century, intensified on the heels of the April 19 uprising. All my comrades and I took deep pride in knowing that it was our role to save our country. As most of us had been trained abroad, we felt strongly the need for early modernization of our country

and, at the same time, we felt that we could utilize effectively the latest techniques of scientific administration
which we had applied in our military careers.

We were confident of our organizing ability and felt
we could carry out any undertaking with close unity, however difficult it might be. With strong traditional nationalism and positive popular support, we saw ourselves as
standard-bearers to guide the people toward the attainment of their long-cherished hope.

chapter three

the takeoff
of the
1960's

The Will To Develop

The successful revolutionaries of May 16, 1961 faced
complex political, economic and cultural problems in
their country. All of them required immediate attention.
But emphasis had to be placed on their plan to construct a
self-reliant economy by revolutionizing industry. Korea
was well aware that this was the key to attaining the revolutionary goal: national reform and reconstruction.

Both the April 19 student revolution and the May 16
military revolution grew out of the chronic poverty of the
nation. They were passionate expressions of the people's
desire to live better. If poverty had been allowed to
weaken them, as had happened before, they would have
faced national collapse. Food comes before politics. Only
with a full stomach can one enjoy the arts and talk about
social development.

Before May 16 the Korean economy was in disorder. Accumulated political blunders and misguided economic policy had utterly disarranged it. The postwar rehabilitation of the nation was at a near-standstill, while the amount of grant-type foreign aid was lessening. Economic stagnation aggravated poverty and unemployment. Farmers' debts rose sharply. On the other hand, a handful of select bureaucrats and business profiteers enjoyed luxury at popular expense. Their over-consumption caused an inflow of foreign commodities, making the nation's balance of payments position severely unfavorable. Syngman Rhee's Liberal Party government in its declining days had lost the opportunity to develop the economy.

The Democratic Party regime which briefly took over power following the April 19 student uprising could not improve the situation, although it announced an economy-first policy. Because of faltering leadership, the climate for economic investment in both government and private sectors took a turn for the worse. As a result, the economy was growing at a rate of only 2.1 per cent, as against a population growth rate of 2.88 per cent.

During the nine-year period after the signing of the armistice in 1953, the per capita national income rose a mere 12 per cent. Even this gain was made chiefly during the rehabilitation period of 1953-1958. With growth at a standstill at the turn of the 1960's, Korea found itself one of the lowest-income countries in the world.

The industrial structure was not solid. Due to a huge gravitation toward them of a huge amount of foreign aid, secondary and tertiary industries seemed excessively swollen in comparison with primary industry. And the

Ulsan Oil Refinery:
Since 1963,
two oil refineries
have been constructed in
joint ventures with
American Gulf and
Caltex concerns.
Now processing 235,000
barrels daily,
the plants supply
not only the nation's need
of fuel for transportation
but also products for
the new petrochemical industry.

of secondary industry contained many unhealthy factors —unbalanced trade, unbalanced development among manufacturing industries, an underdeveloped economic infrastructure and a shortage of industries related to the basic industries, even though the increased amount of value of each industry showed some progress on paper.

U.S. grant-type aid had totaled $2,700 million since the liberation. Yet the Liberal and Democratic Party regimes failed to develop such basic industries as electricity, coal, fertilizer, and cement, and such social overhead capital as roads. They failed also to develop an economic infrastructure involving such sectors as transportation and communications. Private industry could not solve such pressing problems as insufficient facilities, lack of raw materials and financial difficulties because of inadequate government assistance.

As a result, industrial production slowed and the supply of commodities fell far short of the demand. The deficit budget and the misdirected monetary policy increased the amount of money in circulation, stimulating a sharp rise in prices. The economy was faced with collapse.

The institutional and moral aspects of the society were no better. People fatalistically took poverty and reliance on foreign aid as unavoidable facts of life. Businessmen and industrialists failed to fulfill their important role in economic development. Many corrupt government officials and parvenus worked together to amass illegal fortunes. The market, suffering from its small scale and lack of vigorous competition, did not function normally. The underdeveloped agricultural system was unable to meet the demand for food—we were forced to rely on the farm products of advanced countries. The whole economy was afflicted by inexperience, inefficiency and wasteful management.

When I took over power as the leader of the revolutionary group on May 16, 1961, I felt, honestly speaking, as if I had been given a pilfered household or a bankrupt firm to manage. Around me I could find little hope or encouragement. The outlook was bleak.

But I had to rise above this pessimism to rehabilitate the household. I had to break, once and for all, the vicious circle of poverty and economic stagnation. Only by curing the abnormal economic structure could we lay the foundation for decent living standards. But I soon came to realize the difficulty of simultaneously achieving our goals of social stability and economic development, and the goal of efficient government. I was also aware of the fact that economic development in the capitalist manner requires not only an immense investment of money and materials, but also a stable political situation and competent administrators.

To achieve this stability, the military revolutionary government temporarily suspended political activities of students, the press, labor unions and other social and political organizations, which had caused political crises and social unrest during the rule of the Democratic Party regime. We also made it clear that civilian government would be restored in 1963.

Meanwhile, we organized a planning committee of college professors and experts with specialized knowledge

Sunghwan Dairy Farm:
In order to
increase farm income,
the government has encouraged
diversified farming
and has helped finance
cultivation of exportable products,
while endeavoring to
reduce imports of agricultural
products such as dairy goods.

in many fields. By mobilizing the maximum available expertise for government administration and policy-making, we intended to hold in check the arbitrariness and rashness of the military officers. The establishment of this committee served as a turning point. Korean professors began to show positive interest in the realities of the country and to present policy recommendations on the basis of scientific analyses of the country's situation. Even though not all of these recommendations could be justified in terms of efficiency and rationality, their advice was of great help to the revolutionary government. Thus the Confucian tradition of Yi Korea, in which scholars played a positive part in government affairs, seems to have been revived.

The key to improving a backward economy is the way one uses human resources, for economic development is a human undertaking, impossible without combining the people's potential into a dynamic driving force. This task requires not only strong national willpower, but the ability to translate willpower into achievement. Blueprints must be drawn and explained. If people have a sympathetic understanding of a task, they will voluntarily participate in it.

The revolutionary government announced in 1961 the First Five-Year Economic Development Plan (to start in 1962), the first such overall development program ever prepared for Korea. To prepare it, the revolutionary government mobilized all the wisdom and knowledge available and set clear goals, the primary goal being to found a self-supporting industrial economy. The principle of free enterprise and respect for the creativity of private industry was adopted, for in this way we believed that the private sector would be encouraged to act voluntarily. Under the plan, however, the economy was not entirely free, since development of basic industries was directed by the government.

Taking into consideration the structural characteristics of the Korean economy, the five-year plan gave priority to the following things:

1. Development of energy industries such as coal production and electric power;

2. Expansion of agricultural production aimed at increasing farm income and correcting the structural imbalance of the national economy;

3. Development of basic industries and the economic infrastructure;

4. Maximum utilization of idle resources; increased employment; conservation and utilization of land;

5. Improvement of the balance of payments through export promotion;

6. Promotion of science and technology.

In raising funds for these projects, we tried to draw on domestic resources as much as possible. Self-reliant financing was encouraged.

The five-year plan essayed an annual economic growth of 7.1 per cent and a 40.7 per cent increase of GNP during the plan period. It would raise the GNP to $2.5 billion and per capita income to $112 by the target year of 1966, in comparison to $94 in 1960. Exports were to rise to $138 million in 1966, a 420 per cent increase over the base

*The government has helped finance
imports of cattle and breeding stock from Germany,
New Zealand, and Canada to meet the
increasing demand of the domestic market,
as well as to expand dairy farming as a
part of the Development Plan.*

109

year of 1960, improving the international balance of payments. The weight of secondary industry in the industrial structure would increase from 19.4 per cent in 1962 to 26.1 per cent in 1966.

The plan's goal of a 7.1 per cent annual growth rate was then considered almost impossible—unprecedented not only in Kora but also in other developing countries. Some people criticized the plan as too ambitious, but in view of what we needed for future economic development, it was the minimum objective.

Some experts criticized the plan for failing to take into account the possibility of natural catastrophes. Thus, the low agricultural production due to flood disasters in 1962, the starting year of the plan, was an unforeseen blow. Because of this catastrophe the plan did not fully achieve its goals in its early years. But there was no alternative but to push forward—in effect, to try to make something out of nothing.

The past regime had formulated long-term economic development plans such as the five-year plan recommended in the Nathan Report and the Liberal Party's three-year plan. However, these plans all foundered on incompetent administration and the failure of the people to understand their potential benefit. As a result, there was no popular enthusiasm for such efforts. Yet I am convinced that miracles can come from concerted effort and action. If we acted with determination to implement the plan, we could achieve a self-supporting economy and a welfare society in Korea.

Success in the first five-year plan could not immediately bring about a self-reliant economy. It would be only a landmark which the people had to pass on their long, painful journey toward this goal. Indeed, a self-sufficient economy and a welfare society may not be satisfactorily attained during one five-year plan, or even two or more. But what can be begun today must not be put off until tomorrow. This common but everlasting principle underlay our determination. The economy sustained a rapid rate of growth and the industrial structure improved.

We are living today in an era of change and competition. Looking back to the achievements of the past decade, we find that the courage with which we met the challenge of modernizing our country has become our primary motivating force. We met with many difficulties, however, in formulating our policies. Long range policies in themselves were often thought radical by businessmen. Moreover, both the administration and the ruling party lacked knowledge and experience in preparing long-term economic policy, and so we failed to present a clear vision of our policies. Without this vision it is hard to instill confidence. Some policies were hard to execute. For instance, a set of drastic measures taken during the 1960's to raise interest rates, to improve taxation, to liberalize trade, to encourage the introduction of foreign capital and to place the dollar-won exchange rate under a unitary floating system drew much criticism. Still these policies eventually contributed much to the rapid development of the economy.

Of course, the government has sometime made mistakes, though these did not have any major effect on the plan as a whole. Because the government's efforts were

The electronics industry
in Korea has seen
brilliantly rapid growth
during the last
several years.
To develop and encourage
the electronics industry,
the government established a
favorable climate by
means of the Foreign
Capital Inducement Law,
offering foreign investors
a great many incentives
including tax exemptions
and reductions.

112

designed to bring about policy reform, such enterprises as required adaptation to the new pattern of economic activities underwent more than a little inconvenience.

One of our big problems was the shaky foundations of private industry, which was unable to carry its share of the development burden. Furthermore, the market structure was not modernized. Consequently, the government had to play the leading role in the development plan, though we knew well that such a plan must, in the long run, rely on the creativity and initiative of private industry.

In the meantime, the government tried to readjust existing systems to help accumulate private capital, with a view to laying the groundwork of an efficient market competition system. We hoped to encourage businessmen who could play leading roles in planning. On the other hand, rigid restrictions were put on such business activities as ran against these efforts.

The raising of interest rates on both deposits and loans brought a seven-fold increase in bank savings during the ensuing five-year period. Improved taxation enabled the government to formulate a balanced budget. The unitary floating exchange-rate system and trade liberalization sharply increased exports. These all contributed to an increased inflow of foreign capital, to financial stabilization and to the strengthening of the nation's international trading power. We now realize how important these decisions of the past decade were to rapid economic development. Although hard, they were based on objective reality.

To consolidate our past gains, we are now confidently moving forward under the second five-year plan. With this second plan, the economy has greatly expanded its infrastructure and has seen a great development of heavy and chemical industry. The economy is continuing to grow rapidly at this moment.

Groundwork for Self-Sufficiency

In the 1960's Korea changed from a premodern, underdeveloped society to a modern, productive, constantly growing society, moving towards a self-sufficient economy. This was our response to the Development Decade initiated by the United Nations.

High growth rate and structural improvement made the Korean economy a model of rapid progress in the family of developing nations. Many economists, both Korean and foreign, who have studied the process of growth and development which the Korean economy followed during the past decade, observed that the Korean economic development through its two five-year plans compares favorably with the achievements of Germany and Japan, which developed into major industrial nations from the ruins of war, and with Israel, which achieved a nearly miraculous development.

As a result of their experience under the two five-year plans, the Korean people have rid themselves of the pessimism which filled their hearts in the 1950's. Furthermore, the augmented economic power permits us to lessen our dependence on foreign aid and to participate as a bonafide competitor on the world market and an earnest partner of less developed nations, and thereby take part in

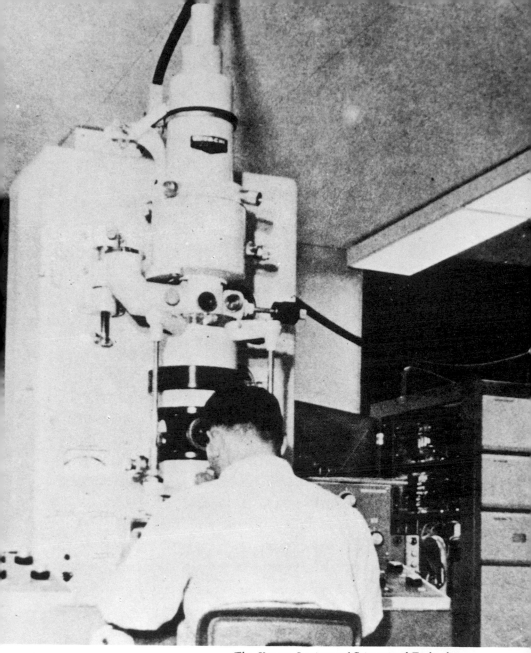

The Korean Institute of Science and Technology laboratories carry out scientific research, surveys and experimentation in industrial engineering and economics, disseminate scientific and technological information, and act as technical coordinator among domestic and foreign research institutions who provide technical service contracts to industry.

the worldwide effort to expand and equalize world economy.

What has the Korean economy achieved in concrete terms? First, the economy grew at an annual average of 8.6 per cent during the past 10 years. This compares with the five per cent set by the United Nations as the goal for annual growth during the first development decade. This engendered a 230 per cent increase in the scale of the economy and a similar increase in national income.

Dividing the 1960's in half, we see the first half registered an annual growth rate of 5.5 per cent, while the latter half recorded an 11.7 per cent growth per annum. Manufactures led this growth, with an annual increase of 16 per cent during the 10-year period. This remarkable development of the manufacturing industry was chiefly due to the great expansion of social overhead capital, which rose by an annual average of 17.1 per cent. During the 10-year period, industrial production, including electric power, rose about five times. Per capita GNP climbed from $95 in 1959 to $196 in 1969.

Second, remarkable structural improvement was achieved. Korea lacks natural resources, but has a large population. Under these conditions, the government had to improve the economic structure by placing greater emphasis on developing the industrial sector, which had been outweighed by the primary industry. Incidentally, technology was to be furthered and foreign markets exploited. Thus the economic policy gave priority to industralization and export of manufactured products. As a result, the share of mining and manufacturing industry in the GNP rose from 14.1 per cent in 1959 to 25.9 per cent in 1969.

Also, the economic infrastructure, including such things as electric power, roads and harbor facilities, was greatly expanded. Both export-oriented and import-substitute industries emerged. In addition, the rapid development of labor-intensive light industries provided a new momentum to exports. Refined oil, cement, steel products, fertilizer, electrical appliances and pharmaceuticals began to be produced at home, thereby greatly saving foreign exchange.

The third and most amazing achievement of the Korean economy in the 1960's was an increase in exports. Because of Korea's small-scale domestic market and our lack of natural resources, the government adopted financial, monetary and industrial policies in support of an export-first principle. Exports grew at an annual average of 42 per cent during the 1960's to bring about a 35-fold increase during the same period. This is the biggest export growth in the world.

As exports were increasing, the composition of export commodities began to switch increasingly to a preponderance of manufactured goods. In 1959, when the total dollar volume of exports was only $20,436,000, 83 per cent of this consisted of raw materials, primarily tungsten, iron ore, dried laver, and fresh fish. In 1969, in contrast, manufactured goods comprised 79 per cent of the total export of $702,811,000. The leading export items in 1969 were plywood, textiles, human hair and wigs. In 1961 Korea exported to only 25 nations; in 1968 to 98. Korean exports to the United States in 1969 amounted to $341,349,100. Thus the exporting industry now holds the position of a driving force for economic development.

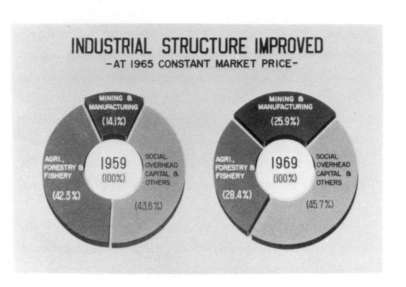

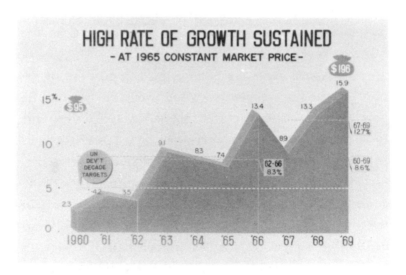

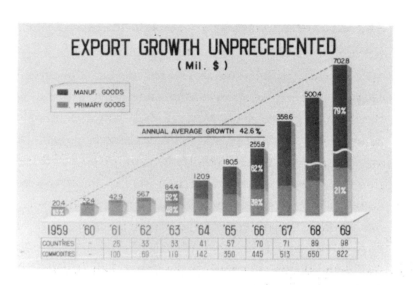

EXPORT GROWTH UNPRECEDENTED
(Mil. $)

MANUF. GOODS
PRIMARY GOODS

ANNUAL AVERAGE GROWTH 42.6 %

	1959	'60	'61	'62	'63	'64	'65	'66	'67	'68	'69
	20.4	32.4	42.9	56.7	84.4	120.9	180.5	255.8	358.6	500.4	702.8
COUNTRIES	-	25	33	33	41	57	70	71	89	98
COMMODITIES	-	100	69	119	142	350	445	513	650	822

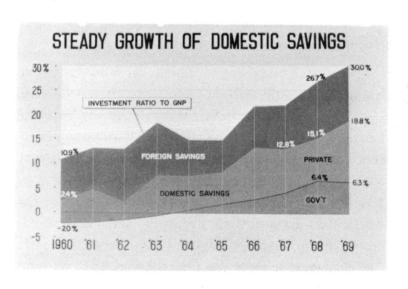

STEADY GROWTH OF DOMESTIC SAVINGS

INVESTMENT RATIO TO GNP

FOREIGN SAVINGS

DOMESTIC SAVINGS

PRIVATE

GOV'T

30.0 %
26.7 %
18.8 %
15.1 %
12.8 %
10.9 %
6.4 %
6.3 %
2.4 %
-2.0 %

| 1960 | '61 | '62 | '63 | '64 | '65 | '66 | '67 | '68 | '69 |

The creative efforts of businessmen to expand their markets contributed to the rapid export growth.

Fourth, the inflation which has chronically threatened the Korean economy was considerably curbed over the 10-year period. This was another major economic achievement. A series of price policies such as a financial stabilization program, a commodity supply-and-demand program, the liberalization of imports, an improved income policy and the elimination of accumulated government deficits helped reduce the annual price rise rate of 20 to 30 per cent during the first half of the last decade to less than 10 per cent during the latter half. Currently, prices are held within the seven per cent rise level. With prices stabilized, the groundwork has been laid for achieving lasting economic stability, a prerequisite to sustained, rapid growth. Stabilized prices also helped normalize market functions.

Fifth, the Seoul-Pusan expressway was opened to traffic to herald the arrival of a transportation revolution. Dedicated on July 7, 1970, the superhighway runs the length of the country. It was constructed with our own resources and techniques. The 428-kilometer-long highway took two years and five months to build, and its cost of $330,000 per kilometer is probably the lowest in the world. The areas coming under the influence of this autobahn-type road hold 63 per cent of the nation's GNP. The vehicles running on this road account for 81 per cent of the total number in operation.

In addition to the Seoul-Pusan and Seoul-Inchon expressways now in operation, construction is underway on a superhighway linking Taejon in the center of the country with Chonju in the south-central region. In 1971 construction will begin on similar highways along the east and south coasts of the country. When these highways are completed, the major economic areas of the country will be within an easy one-day travel distance of each other. This will accelerate urbanization and contribute much to industrial modernization.

When the superhighway program was first pronounced, some people expressed skepticism about it. I said then that expressways would be a better investment of our limited funds than railroads and harbors for solving our transportation bottleneck. The expressways can help to develop industries, to expand the sphere of economic life, and to promote regional development. "This is a project symbolic of our modernization task," I added, "so we must carry it out with our own capital, our own technique and our own effort."

The successful construction of the Seoul-Pusan expressway, the largest civil engineering project ever launched in Korea's history, gave the Korean people a new confidence that they can do whatever they need to do.

In addition, the fivefold increase in bank savings due to interest rate reform, the resulting increment in domestic capital for investment, the doubling of agricultural production, the establishment of a foundation for an improved agriculture, and the construction of an industrial complex at Ulsan on the southeast coast of the country can be cited as encouraging achievements made during the two five-year plans of the 1960's.

The output of
the shipbuilding industry
has increased from
the total annual production
of 49,700 gross tons in 1962
to 160,500 gross tons in 1969.
The industry now
can build steel
cargo ships of the
16,500 gross-ton class.
All the ships built
in Korea are above the
international standard
of A.B.S. in quality.

122

I readily admit that there were several failures in the execution of these plans. There was excessive enthusiasm and too much pressure to attain our goals. We did not accurately evaluate the capital at our disposal, and chose inefficient means of implementing the plans.

The currency reform of 1962 can be cited as the representative blunder of the first five-year plan. This reform was intended to prevent inflation and mobilize idle capital for industrial investment by mopping up excess money in circulation. The result, however, was a drop in the value of the currency and temporary financial confusion.

The measures taken to liquidate usurious loans in rural areas also failed. Designed to cleanse rural society of this obstacle to growth, they attempted to eradicate the centuries-old practice of making private loans at high interest rates. Although a huge amount of money was released to farmers to pay off the usurious loans, the government resorted to coercive methods to re-collect it. Accordingly, the farmers were forced to sell their crops, land and livestock at unreasonably low prices. This caused a sharp fall in farm prices, which hardly helped either agricultural production or income.

The growth-oriented policy of the 1960's caused such important variables as interest rates, the won-dollar exchange rate, tax rates and the money supply to become excessively fixed and rigid. In an economic development policy, these factors must be considered as variables and adjusted flexibly to meet problems. In the 1960's they were not kept flexible enough.

I can see now that errors were made, also, in the methods of fostering of small and medium industry, the introduction of foreign capital and in financial and monetary policies. The government, however, gained valuable experience even through its mistakes in the course of executing the two five-year economic plans.

The development achievements of the Korean economy during the 1960's may seem to some to be either a miracle or an accident. They are neither. They are the result of the will to develop, rooted deeply in the minds of the Korean people; the enthusiastic popular response to the government's policy; the development of education and technology; and the utilization of a skilled labor force.

Efforts Rewarded

Because of limited capital and the shortage of able businessmen, Korea had trouble achieving rapid economic development under a free economic system. In the early stage of this effort, the government had to play the leading role. Efforts had to be made first to improve the government's administrative capability, for without competent administration no successful economic development could be realized.

The politicians of a developing, modernizing, nation should present a realistic policy under systematic leadership. They should not be preoccupied with the pursuit of power or wealth for themselves. Because I felt that our cherished desire for national modernization could not be attained by politicians involved in self-serving political struggles, I decided to organize a political party composed of men with fresh political ideas.

The new 266-mile Seoul-Pusan express
highway was opened in July, 1970, after
two and a half years of construction,
linking the capital with the important
port city of Pusan on the southeastern
tip of the Peninsula. Currently
construction is underway on similar
expressways linking the eastern coast
and southwestern tip of the country,
criss-crossing the Seoul-Pusan route.

In the course of formulating a policy pros and cons can be advanced, but once a policy is decided upon, those who participated in the decision should adhere to it faithfully, whether they approve of it or not. I wanted to see a political party and a parliament composed of politicians who would do this.

Every political idea needs appropriate administrative support. Accordingly, the revolutionary government began immediately to reform the administration of government. There was conservative resistance from established politicians, but by using the advanced management techniques employed in our armed forces, the government was able to carry out this work. Particular emphasis was placed on changing the rigid bureaucracy handed down from the days of Japanese colonial rule into a progressive, efficient system.

Rather than assign new functions to the existing government agencies, we established new organizations to provide effective administrative support for the economic development plan. The Economic Planning Board was established immediately following the May 16 military revolution. This was followed by the reorganization of government economic agencies, including the establishment of the Construction Ministry. Government-run enterprises were also reshuffled. To fulfill effectively its function of controlling and supervising the development plan, the Economic Planning Board was made the highest economic planning agency of the government.

The Office of National Tax Administration was set up to insure fair tax assessment and smooth tax collection. Although the subsequent increase in tax revenue resulted partly from rapid economic development, the fact that tax collections rose by twice the economic growth rate is due to the remarkably improved tax administration. Korea is now ready to formulate its budget with its own revenue, even if foreign aid were to disappear.

To implement administrative reform, a system of planning, review, analysis and control was introduced in all government agencies. But the personnel problem still remained to be tackled. Immediately after the military revolution, the revolutionary government announced a large-scale reshuffle of ranking government officials, except for those serving in fields requiring specialized knowledge and experience. In addition, it established an expensive training program for government officials to equip them with development-oriented management techniques. The early success of this training program was due partly to the cooperation of scholars and government officials.

Government administration was under my direct control, so the reform program there was relatively easy. However, in other areas such as education and the press, it took considerable time to realize the reform plans. These areas resist direct political influence. It was not easy for these sectors, being conservative, to rid themselves of the traditions handed down from Yi Korea through Japanese rule. But in view of the high educational level in Korea as compared with its economic power, the role of education and the press in the national development effort is as important as that of any other sector.

Realizing this, the revolutionary government made an effort to accept their criticism and advice as much as

*On February 7, 1966, during his state visit
to Malaysia, the author met with Prime
Minister Rahman, explained the view and
position of Korea on the Southeast Asian
situation in connection with the dispatch of
Korean troops to South Vietnam, exchanged
views on the collective security of Freé Asia, and
discussed formation of an economic consultative
body to promote economic cooperation and
trade among the Southeast Asian countries.*

128

possible. They were left free to raise objections to the government. However, the government could not avoid taking measures against the revival of the tradition of resistance, originated in the days of Japanese rule and developed under the Liberal Party regime. Opposing for the sake of opposition was neither healthy nor constructive, and it had to be done away with for the sake of national modernization.

One example of this problem was a political crisis caused by student demonstrations against rapprochement with Japan. The political objective of the revolutionary government was to establish a firm national identity and to prevail over Communism. This objective was not an isolationist one, but rather aimed at broad cultural contacts with foreign countries, through a positive open-door policy, so as to receive useful stimulation for national development. It was also meant to increase mutual understanding with other countries and thus promote the international status of the Republic. Above all, it was to speed economic development. Accordingly, the government extended its network of diplomatic missions to neutral nations in Southeast Asia, the Middle East, Africa and Latin America. Exchanges of visits at the head-of-state level were made with several countries, while goodwill missions were dispatched to other countries. As a necessary part of this positive diplomacy, immediate efforts were made to normalize relations with Japan, our nearest neighbor.

Japan's former colonial rule had infused a strong anti-Japanese feeling in the hearts of the Korean people. They could hardly rid themselves of it quickly after the liberation. Moreover, after the liberation stress had been placed on anti-Japanese education, thus intensifying the anti-Japanese attitude. It was inevitable that an attempt at normalizing relations with Japan would draw severe opposition.

I knew that this opposition was motivated by patriotism. However, the force of conservative public opinion could not be allowed to stand in the way of national development. I attempted to convince the people that a changed international situation made normalized relations with Japan a necessity. In spite of my effort, the situation worsened, and a proclamation of martial law was required. This drew intensified criticism from intellectuals and the opposition party. But the government proceeded with its effort toward rapprochement with Japan in view of the far-reaching benefits for the country this was expected to bring.

Parallel with the open-door policy in diplomacy, efforts were made to infuse in the minds of the people a confident sense of national independence. Korea's unhappy past had caused the Korean people to develop a pessimism about life. It must be noted that any non-productive, negative traits of the Korean people are not hereditary; they are the remnants of past invasions and misfortunes. History shows that the Korean people are a hard-working, creative, proud people with a strong sense of achievement. Still, while they were preoccupied with such a negative view, no development effort could bear fruit, however hard the government might try.

The government has worked continually to drive

away this defeatism and revive the national pride. Whenever the occasion has arisen we have called on educators, journalists and other opinion-leaders to play a positive role in leading the people toward national modernization. The government itself has also promoted our sense of national identity by praising the achievements of national heroes.

With the rapprochement with Japan as a turning point, the political situation began to stabilize. Seeing the hoped-for development happening before their eyes, the people began to trust the government.

We steadily enlarged the scope of our diplomacy. In 1965, Korea decided to deploy a contingent of its armed forces in the Vietnam War, the first such action in the nation's history. This decision also split public opinion and it was deliberated by the government for months. But we felt that keeping Vietnam secure from Communism was closely related to Korea's security. The dispatch of our troops would encourage the people of Vietnam in their struggle against Communism. It was a way of repaying those 16 free nations which came to our military aid during the Korean War. And finally, the dispatch of troops to Vietnam was an expression of Korea's confidence in its diplomacy. Korea could no longer be satisfied with the passive diplomacy of merely establishing diplomatic and trade relations with other countries. Economic development and a positive diplomacy both greatly helped promote the sense of national independence.

The Korean people have been used to looking at rulers with a suspicious eye. When I emerged victorious in the 1967 presidential election, enjoying a far greater margin of votes than in the election four years before, I was very happy to have realized my desire to gain the people's confidence through economic development.

Students and intellectuals have begun to modify their antagonistic attitude toward the government. They have come to recognize the merits of the government, while still criticizing its demerits. They have begun to participate in government affairs, sloughing off their past attitude as fence-sitters. This is very encouraging.

Even more encouraging is the fact that the nation is now full of confidence in the future, believing that if one works harder, he can live better. Strong national solidarity has been demonstrated in the unity and courage of the people in facing the series of intensified Communist provocations since 1968.

This unity is also expressed in their faith in democracy. The rising generation born after the liberation is being educated in democracy. It is well aware of today's world situation and it has a sense of mission. The young are confident about their future and we are confident in them.

In order to build a capable new generation, the government drew up a Charter of National Education, formulating an educational policy in compliance with its spirit. Traditionally, the Korean people have had a strong desire for learning, but Korean education in the past lacked objectives. It was not clear as to its purpose. The government, therefore, sponsored a study to establish clear-cut objectives, mobilizing experts in all fields. The result of

The Manila (Philippines) summit conference
of the seven Vietnam War allies
ended on October 25, 1966, displaying
new unity among the free nations in the Asian
and Pacific region and affirming
their joint political, military, and economic assistance
to the Republic of Vietnam and their
concerted efforts to promote international peace.
At this time the author had an
opportunity to consult individually with
President Lyndon B. Johnson and other
heads of state on matters of mutual concern.

133

the year-long study was presented in the form of the Charter of National Education, designed to see that our rising generation should develop both creativity and a sense of cooperation.

We are still in the process of learning how to apply the ideals set forth in the charter to educate children in schools, at home and through the mass media. To achieve self-sufficiency in the foreseeable future, the people must positively participate in national activities in the political, economic and social fields, equipping themselves with a sense of community and a strong national consciousness, rejecting the passive and the pessimistic. While making an effort to achieve peace both at home and abroad, they must move forward toward the national tasks of the 1970's.

chapter four

tides
of the
pacific

The Compass of Peace

Some people see this nation as a danger zone carrying the seeds of strife, or as a powder keg one moment before an explosion. In view of the past 25 years, with their record of division, invasion and open war, these views appear to have some basis.

Twenty years after the cease-fire agreement of July 27, 1953, the Communist threat remains menacing. The infiltration of armed Communists into the Republic, together with the situation arising from the recent U.S. move toward troop reduction here, has led to the fear that more trouble will develop in Korea.

Some specialists find the source of tension in Korea's very geography, as a bridge between island Japan and the northeastern region of Asia. This view can be justified by historical facts. When the Mongols swept southward to Korea in 1231, their ultimate aim was to secure Korea as a base for an attack upon Japan. And when the Japanese invaded Korea in 1592, their intention was to gain a beachhead for advance into the continent.

The Sino-Japanese War of 1894-5 was a struggle between Japan in its effort to advance into the continent and Ch'ing China, which attempted to stop the Japanese from securing a strategic vantage point. The Russo-Japanese War, similarly, arose from a head-on clash between tsarist Russia's march southward and the Japanese march northward toward the Asian continent.

History proves that whenever Korea becomes a battlefield for the powerful, the peace and security of East Asia are at stake. In this sense, Korea holds the key to peace in East Asia. Japan's invasion of Manchuria in 1931 and the outbreak in 1937 of the Sino-Japanese War were cases in point. It may rightfully be said that Japan's launching the Pacific War was predictable from the time of its first advance into Korea.

Consider what happened to Korea after World War II. Korea was divided when Soviet Russia forcibly occupied the northern half of the peninsula. Then, in 1950, came the Communist invasion of the Republic by the Kim Il-sung regime. The peninsula became a bloody battlefield and, even after the cease-fire, a target of Communist aggressive acts.

*The existing steel industry still lacks an
integrated iron and steel mill capable of doing the
continuous work of iron-making, steel-making,
and rolling. In view of the rapid increase in demand
for steel and the development aspect of the
machine industry, the government secured a projected
amount of foreign exchange, in December, 1969,
for construction of an integrated iron and
steel mill whose annual production capacity will be
1,032,000 tons in crude steel when completed
in September, 1973.*

137

But Korea today is quite different from what it was. A solid foundation of national reconstruction has been laid over the ashes of war. Discarding its past as the "Hermit Kingdom," Korea has marched into the world, contributing to the peace and security of the East Asia region.

When Japanese imperialism swept across the Korean peninsula it destroyed the balance of power in this region and, thus, peace in Asia. This ultimately led to the tragic Pacific War. It is clear that if this same peninsula should ever become Communist, peace in the Asian and Pacific region would likewise be seriously threatened. Genuine peace in Asia, especially in northeast Asia, was and is dependent upon peace in the Korean peninsula, and peace in Korea will be secured when our country ceases to be a power vacuum. Korea can fill this vacuum when it builds up its own strength sufficiently to cope with the influence of the big powers. This is the valuable lesson we have learned through our sufferings.

The Korean people's firm belief in the need for the modernization was not derived from self-centered ultra-nationalism. Rather, the enthusiasm for modernization was the outcome of their tremendous effort to live peacefully with all nations in Asia and the Pacific areas. Modernizing our nation is the only shortcut to unification of our divided land, and the most valid means of getting rid of the power vacuum. It is no exaggeration to say that the successful modernization of Korea serves as a compass indicating the direction of peace and security in East Asia.

It is true that in the past the Republic of Korea has

given the unfavorable impression of being an extremely obstinate and inflexible anti-Communist state. But we are trying to present a brighter image to world society. We have even decided to establish friendly trade relations with some countries in the Communist camp. This is a reflection of our desire not to run counter to world trends in this new era of hoped-for detente.

Korea's efforts to ease international tensions have already been demonstrated by its frequent participation in various international conferences, and by the many such conferences held in Seoul. Our leading role in these efforts was exemplified by the Asian and Pacific Council (ASPAC), an international organ established at Korea's initiative. Since its inception in Seoul in 1966, ASPAC has played a great part in promoting understanding and cooperation among the member nations through its annual ministerial, economic, social and cultural conferences, and its importance is rapidly increasing. ASPAC serves as the driving force of the "peaceful revolution" which will enable us to make the Asian and Pacific region a community of nations blessed with peace and balanced in prosperity.

The security of Asia, however, depends above all on the honorable conclusion of the Vietnam War. We feel this acutely, for we sent our troops to Vietnam in the hope of seeing an early and honorable end to this conflict. For even if the Asian and Pacific community is firmly established and the peaceful revolution achieved, our efforts will be in vain if Vietnam and the rest of Indochina become Communist through the free world's acceptance of

In September, 1970,
when an old friend of Korea,
a former member of the
United Nations Commission on Korea,
now the President of
the Republic of El Salvador,
General Fidel Sanchez-Hernandez,
visited Korea,
the author enjoyed
this opportunity to present
a clear-cut picture of the
Korean situation to an expert
familiar with the question.
The two showed
particular interest in the
expansion of economic relations
between the two countries
and agreed in principle
to conclude a bilateral trade pact.

140

a less than honorable solution. If and when the Vietnam war ends with a just peace settlement, our troops will withdraw from the scene without delay.

The Future of Peaceful Coexistence

World politics in the 1960's has been characterized by peaceful coexistence and multipolarity of power.

As the realization deepened that competition in nuclear armament might eventually bring about the near-annihilation of mankind, the prevention of an all-out nuclear war became a new issue directly connected with the national interests of both the United States and the Soviet Union. The changing attitude of these two giants has not only had a great influence on their respective diplomatic policies and military strategies, but has affected all international politics.

In other words, the military bipolarization, with nuclear weaponry as its basis, brought about a multipolarization in international politics. America's worldwide structure of alliances gradually underwent a qualitative change. The United States has now embarked on a search for a new order in international politics suitable to the age of multipolarization.

Some believe that as the nuclear stalemate between the United States and the Soviet Union functions to restrict the involvement of the superpowers in overseas conflicts, newly independent countries will be encouraged

*Prime Minister
John M. Chang,
of the
Democratic Party administration,
announces his resignation
in the wake of
Military Revolution
on May 18, 1961.*

142

to attempt autonomous activity. Countries belonging to the so-called Third World could fish in troubled waters, capitalizing on this trend in international politics while keeping themselves aloof from both side. Others believe that, since nuclear weapons cannot be used in actual warfare, they have already lost political and psychological efficacy and that, therefore, the effect of nuclear armament on international politics is limited to deterrence, and maintenance or strengthening of the status quo.

Fear arising from recent remarkable developments in nuclear weaponry and the reaching of the saturation point in stockpiling of nuclear weapons has led the United States and the Soviet Union to open diplomatic negotiations with a view to easing the armament competition. No notable results have yet been achieved in this direction. Nonetheless, the two powers now exhibit a new tendency of trying to avoid the expansion of, and intervention in, international disputes.

In spite of the interest of the United States and Russia in easing international tensions, however, we must look squarely at the dangers that some parts of the world are still facing. A measure taken to ease tensions in one part of the world could cause or prolong a dispute in another area; self-restraint on the part of the powers for easing tension could promote a multipolarization trend in international politics, giving rise to new international disputes in the peripheral region; a regional dispute may become chronic due to paralysis of the big powers' traditional ability to maintain a power balance—a factor regulating international politics—as both powers, so reluctant to expand the dispute, refuse to interfere.

Even though the progress of peaceful coexistence created a thawing mood in the NATO and Warsaw Pact nations, enabling Western and Eastern European countries to enter into separate diplomatic relations; and, with this development as the background, even though President Nixon's "age of negotiation" seems to have arrived, regional tension still exists in the broad area of East Asia, especially in Southeast Asia. Furthermore, America's disengagement policy as applied to Vietnam is further aggravating the tension. One feature of international politics in Northeast Asia is the fact that the trend to multipolarization is being utilized for its own purposes by the North Korean regime. This presents a sharp contrast to the European region, and negates Nixon's age of negotiation and peace.

Since the Nixon administration came to power, America's foreign policy has sought a new direction—especially as regards East Asia—including the disposition of the Vietnam War. The Nixon doctrine, seemingly reflecting a new isolationist mood arising in the United States, is an effort to avoid excessive U.S. intervention in, and responsibility for, wars—such as the one in Vietnam—that cannot be brought to a successful conclusion by American military power alone. At the same time, it is a move to urge the countries in East Asia, as yet dependent upon America's direct defense support, to step up their own efforts to promote regional security. The problem, of course, is how to fill the power vacuum which will be created in this region if this policy is enforced abruptly.

The Nixon administration promised that the United

*At the invitation of
President Richard Nixon,
the author visited with him
in San Francisco on August 20-23, 1969,
to discuss Korean security,
settlement of the Vietnam War, and the
Okinawa reversion in relation
to Far Eastern security.
The two Presidents agreed on
the desirability of strengthening
existing organizations and
institutions for Asian and
Pacific regional cooperation.*

145

States will discharge its duty as prescribed in the mutual defense pacts concluded with these countries. In other words, the United States is determined to provide the assistance called for in these pacts in case any of its allies in the region are threatened with nuclear war, or are attacked on such a massive scale that they cannot repulse the enemy singlehandedly. However, America will refrain from sending ground forces to the countries in trouble.

As applied to Korea, this doctrine may mean that, even though America will provide adequate support, including a nuclear deterrent, to Korea in case of such large-scale aggression as the 1950 Korean War, or in the event of nuclear attack by Red China, Korea must assume the primary responsibility in coping with other threats such as partial provocations, infiltration, and subversion, initiated by the North Korean regime. Viewed in this light, the Nixon doctrine can be regarded as a reconfirmation of America's promise of defense support and, at the same time, a definition of the boundaries of Korean responsibility.

On the other hand, the doctrine, while emphasizing autonomy and self-help in Asian countries and promising economic and other assistance to them, seems to attach heavy importance to the role of Japan in Asia. The Nixon doctrine presupposes a reevaluation of the economic, political and military potential of Japan, which has now emerged as the world's third largest industrial country.

There is no objection to America's urging self-help on Korea or to its call for the solidification of regional cooperation. However, we must assert that the harmonization of Korea-U.S. and Korea-Japan relations is the key to keeping the Korean peace.

While enforcing the Nixon doctrine, the United States has also made a series of political gestures aimed at easing tension between itself and Communist China.

The de-Americanization policy, so far as Asia is concerned, is likely to undergo many trials and face many problems. Peace in the Far East, including Korea, depends ultimately on the construction of a collective security system strong enough to check any attempts at aggression. In view of our own experience and from precedents found in Europe, we hold that the possession of power is a prerequisite in any confrontation with Communism. Also, it is most necessary to cultivate a correct recognition of Communism.

The Vietnam war started to assume a different aspect in the latter half of 1969. De-escalation is under way and American troop withdrawals are being carried out. At the same time, the de-Americanization and pacification plans are being pushed, in accordance with the Nixon doctrine. Although no progress has been made at the Paris negotiations with North Vietnam, the United States seems determined to resolve all problems according to its previously established plan, regardless of this lack of progress. By the time of the U.S. presidential elections in 1972, the United States plans to have withdrawn about 430,000 troops, that is, the major portion of the American forces stationed in Vietnam.

The ultimate solution to the Vietnam War presupposes a cease-fire, an agreement on the political pattern of Vietnam after the war, international security measures for

The nation's
electric power industry
made great progress
during the 1960's,
with the accomplishment of
the first Five-Year Plan.
Eleven more power plants
are expected to
be completed in 1970-71
when the nation's
total generating capacity
will increase to 3,521 mw
and the rate of the
system spinning reserve
from only 0.9% in 1967
to 26.5% in 1971.

148

Laos, Cambodia and Thailand, and joint international supervision to guarantee the observance of the above agreements. Since the present state of affairs in Vietnam appears too complicated for an early solution to these problems, it is anticipated that the current stalemate will continue for a considerable period of time. The future of Vietnam depends on how effectively the Vietnamese government operates in replacing the American troops with its own troops and in carrying out the pacification plan, and on how firmly the Vietnamese people can unite.

The Vietnam War, however, cannot remain as a problem limited only to the United States and Vietnam. The war is a problem affecting all Asian countries, including Korea, and is critical to world peace. Although Vietnam, Laos and Cambodia are separate, independent countries inhabited by different races, the Communists, as has been shown in the Laotian situation, are operating as a unitary, combined front under the leadership of the Indochinese Communist party, ignoring territorial and racial differences. Therefore, the settlement of a dispute in one area of the Indochinese peninsula is not an ultimate solution. Persistence and strong will are necessary to oppose the Communists until one is found.

That Korea for the first time in its history intervened in a war abroad by dispatching troops to Vietnam was an outcome of its deep understanding of the significance and nature of the Vietnam War. The bravery displayed by more than 50,000 Korean troops dutifully discharging their mission in Vietnam has undoubtedly given strength and encouragement to the dispirited Vietnamese people who are suffering so much from the devastation of war.

The Will to Unification

Some 70 kilometers north of Seoul is a hamlet, an un-heard-of backwoods village which suddenly rose to prom-inence in the summer of 1953, as much a focus of the cold war as Berlin. This village is Panmunjom.

Many tourists from abroad make it a rule to visit this place; they consider Panmunjom a sight to be seen, a place where the unusual atmosphere constitutes a major attraction. To Koreans, however, Panmunjom is a symbol of the nation's tragedy and tribulations. Despite changes in the background and conditions of the cold war, Pan-munjom remains as grim a place as ever; it stands as a re-minder of the national suffering. Panmunjom is the scar of territorial division and national fratricide.

Lying in the middle of the four-kilometer-wide and 250-kilometer-long demilitarized zone that cuts across the Korean peninsula, Panmunjom is the only point of contact and the only avenue of communication between the North and South. But it is a contact point and avenue in form only; in reality, it does not function as such. Both sides are poles apart even while they meet at Panmunjom. All modes of travel and communication are severed be-tween countrymen of common stock, of common history and language; no one knows what has happened to his or her relatives and friends who lived on the other side of this closed gate.

Panmunjom began to attract worldwide attention from the day the guns stopped firing along the Korean War front line. Selected as the truce-signing site, it

President Nguyen Van Thieu
of the Republic of Vietnam,
at the author's invitation,
visited Korea
on May 27-30, 1969.
The two examined
the current situation
in relation to
the Vietnamese conflict,
specifically, the development
of peace negotiations
in Paris; reaffirmed the
policy of the allies
to seek a just and honorable
settlement on the basis of
the joint communique issued
at the Manila Summit Conference
in 1966, and called
President Nixon's eight-point
peace proposal of May 14, 1969,
constructive in pursuit
of peace in Vietnam.

151

emerged as the place of negotiations for a peaceful settlement of the Korean question. At that time, a few leaders in the free world were naive enough to believe that a basis had been established for the peaceful unification of our land. On the contrary, we Koreans were shocked to realize that our long cherished hope for national unification was shattered. And in later years, our dismay and misgiving proved to have been well founded. Our national aspiration for reunification has grown increasingly intense, but the wound of division does not appear any more likely to heal.

The subsequent years did not pass without international or domestic endeavors to bring an end to our tragic division. After the conclusion of the armistice on July 27, 1953, the question of Korea's unification was referred to the Geneva political conference which opened on April 26, 1954. The conference was convened on the basis of a UN General Assembly resolution adopted August 28, 1953, which approved the Korean armistice pact and welcomed the convocation of a political conference under paragraph 60 of the armistice agreement. The Republic of Korea, the 16 UN allies, the Soviet Union, Communist China and North Korea all took part in the conference.

Korea's free allies proffered the following bases for a rational settlement of the Korean question: (1) Acceptance of UN authority in dealing with the Korean question and a major UN role in the settlement; (2) Holding of free general elections in proportion to the population of North and South Korea; (3) Stationing of UN forces in Korea until the establishment of a unified, independent and democratic Korea. These proposals were fully consistent with the principles the United Nations had upheld ever since 1947. Supported by the recommendations of its 16 allies, the Republic of Korea also adopted the same policy of free and general all-Korea elections as its official unification formula. On May 22, 1954, a 14-point Korean proposal was put forward.

Turning a deaf ear to our overtures, North Korean delegates adamantly insisted on their three-point proposal calling for the withdrawal of UN forces, and elections supervised by a commission drawn from neutral nations.

The conference was stalemated, and the 16 Korean war allies issued a joint declaration on June 15, re-stating the joint policy statement they had made in Washington at the time of the armistice. The declaration affirmed the allies' determination to carry out the terms of the armistice and supported the efforts of the United Nations to bring about an equitable settlement in Korea; among other things, the June 15 statement called for genuinely free general elections under UN auspices to achieve a unified, independent, and democratic Korea, and for popular representation in proportion to the population of the two zones.

International efforts in search of a solution to the Korean question moved to the United Nations when the U.S.-U.S.S.R. Joint Commission on Korea, established by the Big Three foreign ministers conference in Moscow on December 27, 1945, broke up. The 2nd UN General Assembly then put the question of Korea on its agenda.

We deeply appreciate and value the UN efforts to solve the Korean question, since the 3rd UN General Assembly in 1948 declared the Republic of Korea to be the

*More than 17 years
after the signing of the
Armistice on July 27, 1953,
the Military
Armistice Commission,
composed of representatives
of the
United Nations Command
and the Communists,
still meet at Panmunjom.*

154

The Yang Di-Pertuan Agong,
King of Malaysia,
visited Korea on April 29-May 3, 1969,
to return the author's
state visit to his country in 1966.
The two shared a firm
and unfaltering belief that
Communist expansionism in Asia should
be countered resolutely
by the united force of all
freedom-loving countries of Asia,
and discussed the enhancement of
mutual economic cooperation
among Asian nations.

155

Prime Minister
John Gorton of Australia
exchanged views with
the author, during the
latter's visit to Canberra
in September, 1968,
concerning the strengthening
of the solidarity of
Asian-Pacific nations on
the basis of the
ASPAC and the 1966
Manila Declaration.
The two also agreed to
explore the possibility of
commercial joint ventures and
to conclude an agreement for
cultural and technical
cooperation between
the two countries.

156

only lawful government in the Korean peninsula. In 1950 the United Nations lost no time in taking military action against the North Korean aggressor. It was the first time a world organization acted to uphold the principle of collective security. On October 7, military action in North Korea was approved, and the UN Commission for the Unification and Rehabilitation of Korea was established. Later, to aid in repairing the ravages of war, the UN Korean Reconstruction Agency was set up. But subsequent efforts at the UN all seemed to run aground.

Before 1960, when the West held an absolute majority in the UN, the question of voting on the Korean unification issue met with no difficulties. But beginning in that year, newly independent Asian and African countries which followed the so-called non-aligned or neutral course of action won admission to the United Nations en masse. They brandished the banner of the "Third World," with its philosophy that international disputes should be settled not with force and politicking but through "normality" and persuasion. Because of this change in the power distribution, the Korean question underwent many vicissitudes at the United Nations. Since the 15th General Assembly, the number of votes supporting the UN resolutions on Korean unification have decreased in inverse proportion to the increase in the number of UN member states.

Proposals for the admission of the Republic of Korea into the United Nations, first submitted by the Republic of China to the UN Security Council on December 8, 1955, were repeatedly defeated by Soviet Russia's veto. Therefore, the question of Korean unification was approached from a different angle. Each year, only the representative of the Republic of Korea was invited to the UN debate on the Korean question.

Then U.S. Ambassador Adlai Stevenson submitted an amendment calling for the invitation of a North Korean delegation to the UN debate on the Korean question, provided that North Korea first recognize the "authority and competence" of the world body to deal with the Korean unification issue. Since that time, the question of the North Korean invitation has become an important procedural issue in addition to the unification question itself.

That was not all. A type of delicate hedging gradually came to the fore. The Indonesian delegate proposed to the 16th General Assembly that "as a new approach to the solution to the Korean question, an international conference of the countries concerned be held in a neutral place such as Geneva under the sponsorship of the United Nations." At the 18th General Assembly, Indonesia suggested a way of breaking the deadlock by proposing that the question be solved through direct negotiations between South and North Korea, under the sponsorship of neutral countries, outside the United Nations. At the 17th General Assembly, Canada suggested that U.S. forces stationed in Korea be replaced by troops of non-aligned neutral nations and the UN Commission for the Unification and Rehabilitation of Korea (UNCURK) be reorganized in a way acceptable to both the South and North Korean governments. Iraq called for the "convocation of a special conference which will strive to find a consensus on Korean unification." Tunisia and Ceylon expressed the opinion that "in view of the fact that the settlement of the Korean problem has been impossible with the measures

*Korea joined the
International Telecommunications
Satellite Consortium (INTELSAT)
and opened an
earth station in Keumsan,
on June 2, 1970, to
transmit and receive messages
through international
communications satellites.*

159

worked out in the past, the General Assembly must recognize a new means of solution."

The proposals of some neutral nations became more outspoken at the 22nd General Assembly. These countries joined forces with Communist countries in submitting plans for the simultaneous invitation of South and North Korean delegates, the withdrawal of the UN forces, and the disbandment of UNCURK. They proposed a conference of the countries concerned and the omission of the Korean question from the UN agenda.

To make matters worse, some free world allies, even some that had fought during the Korean War under the UN flag, demonstrated an increasing lack of interest in the Korean question. British Commonwealth countries—Australia, Canada and New Zealand, for example—spoke against the automatic General Assembly meeting. On August 11, 1966, Chile gave notice of her intention to withdraw from UNCURK. Pakistan, another member, also expressed her wish to withdraw. Some Korean War allies withdraw from the group of nations that had jointly submitted the UN resolutions on Korean unification—France and Greece at the 20th General Assembly, and Turkey at the 21st. Canada announced its intention of doing the same thing.

The fact remains that the United Nations, supported by the world's conscience, has made a continuous effort for more than two decades to work out a solution to the question of Korean unification. Korea has maintained solid relations with the United Nations throughout. It was on these good relations that we Koreans pinned our primary hopes for territorial reunification, but this does not mean that we failed to work toward this end ourselves. The fact is that our persistent unification efforts have not yet made any marked progress because of the barriers thrown in their way.

The most serious obstacle is Kim Il-sung and his followers, who still control the northern half of the Korean peninsula.

Calculating each turn of events, the Communists keep repeating their favorite slogans, such as "peaceful unification," "South-North negotiation," "a federal system," "South-North exchange" and even "assistance to the South."

Whenever Kim Il-sung and his party have indulged in various criminal acts, they have unfailingly opened a peace offensive before and after their atrocities. Their first "peace offensive," as I noted, was designed to camoflage the invasion of 1950. On June 25, 1949, the "Fatherland Unification Democratic Front" was formed in Pyongyang, allegedly with the participation of 71 political parties and social organizations of both North and South Korea. The front immediately proposed a five-point unification formula, which included provision for general elections in both North and South Korea, as well as the evacuation of foreign forces. Less than a year later, Kim Il-sung provoked the Korean War.

Kim, who since the armistice had advocated general elections in South and North Korea under the supervision of neutral nations, suddenly in the 1960's began to preach autonomous peaceful unification under the so-called "three-stage unification formula." The first stage called

*President Chiang Kai-shek
of the Republic of China
received the author in
Taipei, in February, 1966.
The two reaffirmed
the traditional ties of friendship
existing between their countries,
agreed upon mutual
cooperation to the maximum in
pursuit of common goals,
and recognized the urgent
need of helping the
South Vietnamese people.*

162

for the withdrawal of the U.S. forces from South Korea, the conclusion of a non-aggression and peace treaty between South and North Korea, the reduction of armed forces in each sector below the 100,000-man level and the commencement of economic and cultural exchanges. At the second stage, according to Kim's blueprint, a federation would be formed with each side maintaining its own political and social structure, and a "supreme national commission" would be established with representatives from the two governments. The third stage would witness general elections to be held throughout Korea to form a "unified central government" without the intervention of foreign influence. The unification formula was cannily designed to promote confusion in the South by stirring up the sentimentality harbored by people about unification, and by capitalizing on the rapidly changing international situation and the chaos caused in South Korea due to the April 19, 1960 student uprising. At the same time, his move aimed at influencing world opinion to the disadvantage of South Korea. In the latter half of the 1960's, as the Republic of Korea's development became more conspicuous and its anti-Communist posture became stronger, the Communists changed their attitude. Once more they switched to the theory of revolutionary unification. With the dispatch of a commando team to Seoul on January 21, 1968, Kim Il-sung stripped off his mask of peaceful negotiation.

Busy with war preparations for the past 10 years, Kim's cadres have completed the fortification of all North Korea, the armament of the entire population, and the militarization of the party. Watching his chance to reinvade, Kim now publicly announces that the early part of the 1970's is the decisive moment for unification by arms. This is the appalling barrier hampering unification.

Yet, no matter how steep and rugged the road to unification may be, we affirm that we must settle the question by peaceful means. It should be made crystal clear that the Republic of Korea has not the slightest intention of seeking unification by war.

What should be done, however, if Kim Il-sung does not abandon his ambition of unifying the country by force and provokes a second Korean War? We will not take a single step backward. Should such a war occur, all the people, soldiers or civilians, will fight to the very end.

However, we do not want such an emergency to occur. It is our firm belief that the big prerequisite for peaceful unification is to ease the present state of tension existing between South and North Korea. We are also firmly convinced that if Korea is to be unified by democratic means, democratic general elections must take place first under the guarantees and supervision of the UN, representing world opinion.

Accordingly, if Kim Il-sung desists from any sort of military provocation, including the dispatch of armed agents into the South, and makes a public announcement that he renounces the policy of communizing the whole of Korea by force; if we can recognize that the North Korean Communists are proving their sincerity with deeds and the United Nations verifies this, we would be prepared to suggest realistic means to lay the groundwork for unification—always, of course, on the basis of humanitarian considerations.

*After the first
oil refinery was completed
at Ulsan in 1964,
the Honam Oil Refinery
was built in 1968,
near Yosu Harbor, as a
joint venture between Honam Oil
of Korea and Caltex of the U.S.
The Ulsan refinery is
a joint venture between
the Korea Oil Corp. and
Gulf Oil of the U.S.*

We would earnestly consider the gradual removal of artificial barriers existing between the two parts of Korea which presently block commerce, postal service, and traffic, and the opening of doors to mutual exchanges in the fields of education, culture, the arts, sports, the press, and science.

If the North Korean regime recognizes the United Nations' efforts for democracy, unification, independence and peace in Korea and accepts its competence and authority in this regard, we would not be opposed to the presence of the North Korean Communists at the UN deliberation on the Korean question.

However, I do not expect the North Korean Communists to meet these prerequisites in the foreseeable future. As has been proved by such acts as the capture of the USS Pueblo on the high seas and the downing of a U.S. EC-121 reconnaissance plane over international waters—to say nothing of the Korean War itself—the North Korean Communists are trying to create a feeling of danger on the Korean peninsula to maintain their own power. Therefore, so long as Kim Il-sung remains in power in North Korea, I do not believe the tensions now gripping the Korean peninsula can be eased.

Does this, then, rule out any chance for peaceful unification in the near future? I am not pessimistic about this problem. I strongly believe that a breakthrough will soon come. Liberalization will eventually affect North Korea. The liberalizing trend in the Communist world is, I believe, so great a force that it cannot be held in check by any one dictator, however powerful he may be.

Should Kim Il-sung's dictatorship become shaky in

the face of this irresistible force, the North Korean Communists would inevitably give up their illusion of communizing the whole of Korea by force, and opt for a peaceful means of unification. In such a situation, major efforts for the peaceful and democratic unification of Korea could be made and steps toward this goal would be taken one after another.

I hope that, when the time comes, our national strength will have grown and international conditions will have ripened so as to aid our efforts in this cause. The key to unification lies in how much the liberalization process in North Korea can be internally advanced and ultimately directed.

We are earnestly waiting for the arrival of such a time. But in the meantime, we must carry on a bona fide competition that can show the North Korean Communists that democracy provides a better living for the people than Communism. To this end, we must make a continued effort to promote our freedom and expand our prosperity.

I am also sure that Kim Il-sung's plan of communizing the whole of Korea by force will fail, for such a plan runs against the traditional philosophy of the Orient. In the Orient, political philosophy has from ancient times been based on the virtue of benevolence, a virtue which calls for charity and comprehension and completely renounces force and violence. Benevolence is still rooted deeply in the consciousness of the Korean people and exerts an important influence on their ways of thinking. Benevolence still remains an indispensable qualification of a leader. I hope that someday Kim Il-sung and his followers may re-

Emperor
Haile Selassie I
visited the author in Korea
in May, 1968,
furthering Korean-Ethiopian relations,
already forged on the
Korean War battlefields.
As initiator of the
Organization of African Unity,
the Emperor has helped
Korea stretch its
friendly arms to the
African continent in search
of more friends among
non-aligned nations.

168

cover this Oriental virtue, and their national consciousness as Koreans. But the likelihood is not great.

Koreans have overcome many national crises with vitality and perseverance. They should take pride in their spiritual heritage of optimism and in their resistance to despair. Many ordeals will lie along the road to national unification, but with the vitality of our ancestors we must carry out this historic mission. We must continue our march forward to unification, entertaining hope and confidence, and displaying courage and patience. We must cross over the mountains lying ahead of us in our march, however steep they may be. For the bright morning of unification will surely dawn soon.

chapter five

we shall not give up halfway

The Continuing Challenge

We are now living in the age of national revitalization, in which all of us are called upon to liquidate our unfortunate past, renounce the mistakes of our history and strive for national revival with renewed resolution. Our past experiences have led us to pursue our ideals with devotion. Our sufferings have led us to a zeal for construction.

Our goals are quite clear. They are to establish a politically independent, sovereign state; to build a prosperous society in which all are guaranteed a decent economic life; to enable all to live with pride, wisdom and love through the further promotion of national culture; and to bring freedom to the people in the lost half of our land by reunifying the divided country.

In order to complete these tasks, we must single out various factors that impede our advance. Rational persuasive measures will be needed to channel the people's

Shinjin Motor Company
is one of the
four motor vehicle manufacturers,
all started since 1962.
At this stage, however,
the Korean automobile industry
is still limited to
assembling of knock-downs.

strength into the national endeavor, and to overcome negative factors. The advance toward these ideals will be in every case challenged by rugged adversaries, some of them unlooked for. But with composure, we must tackle them one after another.

The contemporary world economy is in a state of unprecedented confusion. It is inevitable that the Korean economy, now in the process of transition to a free-economy system as a result of a high growth rate, will relate closely to the world economy. It is presumed that our pace of growth, and the character and direction of our development will be greatly affected.

The equilibrium of the world economy is being shifted fundamentally by such phenomena as uncertain business conditions and the deflation policy in the United States, which is connected with the de-escalation of war in Vietnam; by excessive protectionism and a lack of sincerity on the part of advanced countries in solving the problems existing between the "have" and "have-not" nations; and by the highly competitive industrialization policies of advancing countries as they change from raw material suppliers to processing countries. We have also the trend in the direction of trade blocs and the insecure international financial market. All these constitute grave challenges to the future of the Korean economy, which depends largely on exports, on imports of raw materials, and on the introduction of foreign capital as prerequisites for maintaining a sustained high growth rate.

In our fight to counter these external challenges effectively we plan to: (1) strengthen economic cooperation with neighboring countries, with the ultimate goal of co-ordinating development programs and establishing a common market; (2) pursue common development programs through joint investment with major raw-material-supplier nations, and (3) expand the scale of industrial plants, advance technology and promote labor productivity as a means of improving our nation's international competitiveness.

Four major problems may require action at home. First, the balance of international payments situation may become serious. This is attributable to financial pressure on the country's trade, arising from the increased demand for basic raw materials and intermediate materials to supply the industrialization program and export drive. Also, consumption has increased with rising incomes and urbanization. When we think of the need to repay debts to foreign capital suppliers, the improvement of the international payments situation remains one of the most urgent tasks to be accomplished if growth is to continue.

Second, it must be conceded that our drive to attain a high growth rate and develop strategic sectors with limited resources and capability have brought about an undesirable imbalance in the Korean economy. The imbalance is especially noticeable in the differences in income level and development progress between agricultural and urban regions, resulting from rapid urbanization and industrialization. There is an unhealthy gap between large and small enterprises, and between people in the high-income and low-income brackets. From the long-range viewpoint, such an imbalance might be called growth toward a new equilibrium. Or it might be viewed as the birth

*Tongnip
Industrial Company
on the
outskirts of Seoul,
produces 450,000 tons
of flour, sugar, starch,
and alcoholic
spirits annually.*

174

pains of development. As part of our endeavors to create a modern, consistent economic structure, we will do our utmost to implement new broad-gauge policies to correct this imbalance. They include, for example, a reform of the taxation system, a national campaign to raise earnings of farmers and fishermen, relocation of industrial facilities to rural areas, expansion of community development programs, and development of small and medium industry.

Third, we succeeded throughout the 1960's in laying a solid foundation for economic growth by investing enormous amounts of capital and labor in the expansion of social overhead capital such as electric power, communications, ports, and transportation facilities. Yet the social overhead sector was still unable to keep pace with the overall growth rate, because resources were limited and capital demanded in competing sectors. This emerged as one of the factors restricting the greater acceleration of industrial production and the faster growth of exports and investment. Stepped-up efforts will be made during the third five-year plan period to eliminate bottlenecks arising from the shortage of social overhead capital. We must build a firm base for fast economic growth and a self-sufficient economy.

Fourth, the weak management of Korean private enterprises is another major problem. Among developed and developing countries, private enterprises take the initiative in expanding the economy once the primary development plan period is over. The role of government is to maintain for private enterprise conditions under which it can engage freely in economic activities, and to guarantee fair competition. Government must keep down its intervention by restricting its economic activities to extremely strategic sectors. The remarkably rapid economic growth of the Federal Republic of Germany and of Japan, and the introduction of the principle of free competition in some East European countries, are illustrations of the desirability of this arrangement.

At the outset, the Korean economy followed a government-oriented pattern. In the mid-1960's an attempt was made to transform it into a private business-oriented economy with the implementation of realistic, liberalized economic policies. Contrary to the original intention of our economic planners, however, private businesses are not yet able to play their full role according to modern business standards, and so are still a drag on economic development.

The deficiencies of private enterprises include their small scale and inefficiency due to the limited domestic market, their weak financial structure, the family ownership system, and a lack of creative management. In a free, competitive society, it goes without saying that economic development is attainable when the private sector is enlightened and is encouraged in taking the lead. We need a dynamic, voluntary campaign for managerial reformation in private enterprise.

These are not the only problems. As our economy grows toward self-sufficiency, many others will press upon us. Rapid industrialization may require more manpower. The demand for capital will continue to move upward, as will prices. The development of defense-related industries will become urgent, if economic development is to be maintained while we disburse enormous sums for military

*Besides the introduction of heavy agricultural
machinery such as tractors and combines,
smaller scale machinery to meet peculiar
farming conditions has been developed since the
beginning of the first Five-Year Plan period.
The production of modern equipment such as
power tillers, power sprayers, etc., has
gradually increased, and by 1963, Korea began to
export some of them to Southeast Asia.*

177

expenditures. The influx of foreign agricultural goods may necessitate action to protect the people from undue financial burdens. The reform of the agricultural structure and the acceleration of an agricultural revolution will be absolutely necessary in order to attain a self-sufficient economy. Other problems will include the establishment of fair, effective competition; the encouragement of technical renovation; and the prevention of overpopulation, public nuisances and housing shortages in urban areas.

Such challenges do not dishearten us. Instead, they make us stronger. By profiting from the lessons learned through hardships, we are determined to advance, before this decade ends, to the goal of a completely self-sufficient economy and a welfare society in which the people are assured of an adequate living, the improvement of the environment and of labor conditions, and a fairer distribution of income.

I believe strongly that the North Korean Communists pose the gravest possible challenge to the successful accomplishment of our national goals. The more our economy develops, the more our people take pride in being members of a free society, strive to enhance their cultural heritage, and aspire with confidence for territorial unification, the more the North Korean Communists may grow impatient, and so try to create tension in the Korean peninsula. But we shall vigilantly maintain a strength and a mobility powerful enough to counter any North Korean challenges.

When I look at the realities of international politics, I fully understand that the gathering clouds are not only arising from the Communist world but also from among some of our friends. There is always competition and confrontation of conflicting national interests in the relationship of countries. Because of this, I predict that many difficulties with foreign countries will arise. This will become increasingly true as we bring our economy closer to self-sufficiency, as we take action to secure our political independence, and as we move toward the national goal of reunification.

We have in our hearts and minds the courage born of history, which will enable us to reject any relationship that is not established on mutual trust but instead coerces us to accept economic subjugation, political control or ideological regimentation. At the same time, we must pay keen attention to the possibility that challenges to our advance may come from our own rank and file. Moving toward difficult goals is always accompanied by swift changes and reforms. There exists a constant danger of a division in national public opinion, unless we create a climate of dialogue with reason and exercise thoughtfully our power of judgment regarding the common goals of our nation.

My primary objective is to strengthen the forces of independence within society. Hence, I appreciate well-meant competition and criticism which make a positive contribution to social development. But I am also aware that unproductive confusion can arise, under the pretext of liberty, to the detriment to our advance toward national modernization. What should worry us most is the appearance of a climate in which healthy standards of criticism give way, common ideals are forgotten, and

Reverence for scholarship has been traditional in Korea, but never has education been attempted on such a large scale and so earnestly in Korea as in recent years. Now special emphasis is placed on qualitative development at all levels of education, in view of the fact that the accelerated quantitative growth of education has been achieved. In fact, the rapid development of Korea is largely due to the universal high level of education among its populace.

common sense is disregarded as various interests are given priority.

It is my firm conviction that disunity at home should be prevented in advance with wisdom, patience and self-control. I should like to emphasize that democratic ways of forming public opinion, operating not through dogmatism or self-righteousness but through debate and persuasion, should be set in motion, respecting always the people's right to express their thoughts freely, and lending a receptive ear to productive and constructive opinions. In this spirit, I ask all the people to abandon factional strife for the sake of achieving the common goals of our national advancement.

The Enhancement of National Identity

The urge to economic development that consistently characterized our national life throughout the 1960's has brought about brilliant results in a once-barren land. They have become important milestones in our national march. Our people have recovered their enthusiasm, in their search for something useful. They believe in the future. Many people have rediscovered their treasured individual potential in the execution of government policy. The rising tendency to cooperate is felt everywhere around us. The capabilities of those in charge of administration and management have improved markedly.

New industrial complexes not only create new manufactured goods but also produce a confident and proud people. The educational system produces able, progressive young intellectuals and plays a key role in the formation of national morals by planting in the hearts of people a burning desire to develop their country. The same is applicable to the rural people. Actually, farmers benefit less from the modernization program than the urban populace, yet they are making unflagging efforts to improve land and labor productivity. They seek better cultivation methods and improvement of seed in government community development projects. Our farmers further demonstrate their persistent will to raise their living standard through various self-help projects such as side jobs or off-season work.

Since no change can take place without the voluntary participation of citizens, one could not exaggerate the importance of the modern Korean self-awakening. We are now on the very threshold of a welfare society with the beginnings of a self-supporting economy. However, we are not satisfied with today's reality. We want to help less developed countries when our national wealth puts us in the level of semi-advanced countries, *i.e.,* when all Koreans have a fairly equal share in economic benefits.

We firmly believe that the fundamental basis of our goals is found in the construction of a prosperous country and in our dedication to world peace and prosperity. But the ideals of man are by no means limited to the satisfaction of economic desires. We would not hesitate to live a life of poverty, if a life of luxury would mean subjugation. Our aspiration to attain a self-sufficient economy arises from a thirst for national identification. In my book, *The Country, The Revolution And I,* I interpreted the *hongik*

The author in the field on a harvest day.

ingan, the fundamental ideal of our national foundation, as the creation of a free and independent Korea in which simple, diligent, honest, ordinary citizens constitute the backbone of the state—a society of ordinary citizens in which all are guaranteed a free, prosperous, peaceful life with a high level of culture. Starting with the reform of our economic society, we aim to restore our independence and bring about a cultural revolution through the process of self-discovery on the part of every man. The eventual goal of modernization will be achieved only with the modernization of each human being.

In the modernization of advanced countries, national leadership put emphasis on spiritual reform prior to economic change. Modernization efforts bore fruit only after the energy of a nation was effectively integrated into a single objective by superb leadership from above. In the case of Korea, this modernization process was reversed. Because the emancipation of the people from poverty was most urgent, we began with economic development. But this did not mean that we forgot the need for the balanced improvement of people's lives, the enhancement of ethical values, the prevention of human degradation and the establishment of sound intellectual life.

While our economic foundation was being put into good shape, I proposed an ethical code of conduct and exhorted the people to follow this code in their daily lives. My intention was to help establish the spiritual underpinnings necessary for the creation of a brighter society. For I realized that no purely welfare society would be able to function without a spiritual revolution, or without diligence, thrift, self-support and mutual assistance.

Hongik ingan is the basic slogan by which our ancestors explained such a need in a most concise but appealing manner. We embodied this ideal in the Charter of National Education, which advocates the formation of creative, enterprising and patriotic human beings.

The creative man should accomplish the sublime mission of national modernization by using the proud scientific, cultural and artistic heritage received from our ancestors, linking our wisdom and sagacity and our own spiritual posture with the spirit of the Western pioneers. This is my personal ideal for the individual citizen and the growth of his originality.

By enterprising man, I mean to stress the need for building a systematic organization on the principle of mutual help that has been part of Korean life from ancient times, although it is not unconnected with the Western ethic of efficiency. This type of man aims at making productive use of good human relations with a view to materializing, in the modern sense, our traditional ideal of national cohesiveness and the spirit of magnanimity.

Patriotic personalities, with a deep-rooted spirit of resistance against intrusion from outside and a strong love of the nation, should absorb and develop the concepts of citizenship and public service which were the main force of Western nation-building. A new model man should logically develop from a nation which desires to revive cherished national sentiments, which has survived privation so heroically, and which seeks to protect and enhance the freedom of the individual.

Creativity, cooperation, and patriotism are the supreme aims of life and the major premises on which to

Tiger:
A Painting of
the Yi Dynasty,
attributed to
Sim Sa-jong
(1707-1770).
Vertical scroll,
ink and color
on paper.
Height
38-3/8 in.,
width 22-1/16 in.
National
Museum of
Korea.

build a value system. They are also the basic values of our historic inheritance. In short, they are *hongik ingan.* They are the spirit of *hwarang* revivified.

It is fortunate to see a consciousness of the need to defend our political as well as our economic independence arising within our society. We must make a thorough, sincere study of our national consciousness, impelling our people to contribute to the national development. As long as we believe economic construction is not an end in itself, but a necessary and essential condition to attaining national ideals, we shall strive to preserve and enhance our political sovereignty through the popular will.

The Pride of a Cultured Nation.

Orientals possess a mysterious, unified and harmonious spiritual culture that can scarcely be understood completely by Westerners, who have different ways of thinking and different systems of logic. Although it is risky to generalize, it is clear that Oriental cultures have a certain gentle, mild rhythm and harmony. This characteristic is all the more conspicuous in the culture of a nation with a long history. The 4,000 years of Korean history are the reservoir of our endless national pride, the product of accumulated wisdom that cannot be made or altered overnight.

Our ancestors did not simply imitate the cultures of Asia, but absorbed them with a sense of national identity. The Yi Dynasty's *Songrihak,* which expounds a profound theory of human nature and the rule of heaven, is an excellent example of the superb power of Korea's theoretical imagination. Koreans developed a far more original academic theory than did their Chinese teachers. For we did not regard man and heaven as being opposed to each other. We took it for granted that they coexisted in one harmonious celestial body. This viewpoint produced a peculiar ethic for the ruler and ruled in Korea, according to which public sentiments were believed to represent heavenly feeling. Moderate ways of thinking—searching for the basic sources of social development and progress in justice and reason—constituted the keynotes of our philosophy.

While adapting their lives to the social order, Koreans thought it ideal that the order be kept peacefully and developed on a higher dimension. They did not believe that conflicts and contradictions in their society were to be solved largely through struggle and adjustment, as was the case with European nations. Instead, they thought that virtue and tolerance within the limits of the will of heaven solved conflicts and contradictions. Each Korean was proud of his existence in a society where all members were closely tied together by deep affection and respect.

Thus we maintained human relations characterized by mutual trust, honesty and justice. The highly cultured personality of Koreans and their moral standards were an example to others. The typical Korean had high esteem for his morality. He was a man of integrity who pursued a moderate course of action and loved peace and serenity. Koreans were admired by the Japanese, Chinese and

A Girl at the Pond:
A Painting of the Yi Dynasty,
by Shin Yun-bok (1758-?).
Album leaf, ink
and color on silk.
Height 11-7/8 in., width 9-7/8 in.
National Museum of Art.

neighboring Asians. We were given the nicknames of "The Country of Courtesy in the East" and "The Land of the Morning Calm."

This Korean way of thinking slowed down the formation of the individual ego, in a modern sense. Ignorance of material civilization hindered technological and scientific development. Yet, what we lost in the world of machines we gained in the world of the arts and the spirit.

Of all our inventions, Hangul is the gem. The Korean alphabet is a surprising product of Korean culture and remains its best symbol. It is one of the most rational alphabets in the world, in that the shapes of the 24 phonetic signs indicate the manner of their articulation. In proper combinations, it can be written either vertically or horizontally. It is, in short, a convenient, superior alphabet and has been adapted to the typewriter. For Koreans, who have always lived within the Chinese cultural sphere, the invention of Hangul was an epoch-making event. We also take great pride in the fact that Hangul is not for a select aristocratic group, but for all the people.

The past century witnessed assaults on this brilliant culture. Western thought and technology, which began to be introduced when Korea adopted an open-door policy in the 1870's, came as a shocking blow to most Koreans. But more serious was the later attempt by the Japanese colonialists to destroy Korean culture. Because of this attempt, our culture came to contain fragments of things Japanese, whether we liked it or not. By the time of our national liberation in 1945, a considerable part of the culture had become distorted. It was around this time that the tide of Western ideas and customs hit our land with full force.

Individualism and democracy, which were brought to Korea along with Western civilization after 1945, were accepted by Koreans who were grateful for the liberation and felt friendly toward the West. These new ideologies began to exert a sweeping and far-reaching influence on our institutions and ideology. A tendency arose to shift the blame for our past national humiliation to the traditional culture. Some cynically held that the stagnation and retardation of the past were due to the meditative, serene inertia that characterized Oriental culture. Undeniably, the newly independent country took much of its traditional culture to be a stumbling block to the building of a liberal democratic state. The traditional Korean way of thinking hardly guaranteed individual freedom, insured equality of all, or recognized basic unalienable rights.

Various alien social forces unleashed simultaneous attacks on our traditional culture. Inferior elements of Western culture did much to ruin the graceful Korean lyricism that forms the undercurrent of traditional culture. Communist elements determined to wreck the national traditional culture once and for all. In these circumstances, the new wave of idealism was betrayed by bitter and painful reality. The territorial division and the Korean War were terrible shocks, as was the emergence of an undemocratic, autocratic regime in the postwar era.

Our traditional culture exposed its negative side, which was subject to criticism on the grounds of stagnation, indolence and unreality. The more acutely people felt the gap between ideals and reality, the more strongly

From the ashes
of the Korean War,
the city of Seoul
has risen as a modern metropolis
within a decade.

192

was tradition considered an unacceptable remnant of the premodern heritage. Corruption and injustice were often regarded as parts of this heritage. The lethargic spiritual posture of the ruling elite was mistakingly seen as part of its traditional image, instead of individual corruption and incompetence.

When revolutionary ideas on social improvement began to sweep the country in 1961, I spelled out my views on nationalism in an effort to preserve Korea's cultural and spiritual independence. I did so with the firm conviction that we must overcome our self-torment and must imbue individuals with a sense of pride. We needed re-discovery of our national wisdom and renewed pride in our traditions.

Since then I have devised many institutional guarantees in the hope of bringing about the rejuvenation of the national culture and the development of new traditions of our own. The government erected statues of our great national leaders across the country. A sanctuary was dedicated to Admiral Yi Sunsin, who heroically defended the country from the Japanese invasion in the 16th century. By linking the past with the present, we tried to interpret our history in such a way as to present vividly the tenacity with which Koreans through the ages had maintained their lives in the midst of travail.

The effects of this effort are already visible. It seems to me that, in their cultural tradition, Koreans have slowly begun to discover what it means to be a Korean. They are beginning to realize that the traditional culture is a productive force in itself in the process of modernization, contrary to the general belief in the past. Furthermore, our people have now come to possess a sense of mission. They see themselves as developers of a cultural heritage already full of unique aesthetic values and wisdom. Korean studies has become a vital academic subject. A search for a new socio-psychological approach is also being made.

Our task is to accept, resolutely and decisively, the good aspects of newly introduced foreign cultures and make them ours, attaching them to the foundations of the traditional one. We should not automatically reject the rational, efficient cultures of advanced countries. New cultures are created only through constant contacts and exchanges with neighbors. Foreign cultures have made great contributions to our daily life, and we should begin to incorporate contemporary world currents into our tradition. But they must be assimilated positively and productively.

It is urgent that we pay the utmost attention to the possibility that our culture could be destroyed. We must so restructure it that foreign cultures will not dominate us and threaten our heritage. Around us, I feel a strong trend in this direction. We have already decided to use Hangul exclusively. Under a long-range education program, we shall encourage a spirit of creativity by reforming education. The tradition of mutual help, bolstered by fidelity and love, has begun to find its place in the people's consciousness. The creative abilities of individual citizens are developing remarkably. In the arts, Koreans' aesthetic sensitivity is bringing about a graceful revival.

The creativity and wisdom inherent in the Korean people are affecting all walks of contemporary life. No

From a train windo
the author views rural conditio
on one of numerous fact-finding tr
to all parts of Kore

longer do people regard our heritage, so rich in tradition, as something obstinate, premodern and unscientific. They have begun to realize that it can create as well as conserve. In the next few years, our work to effectuate a spiritual revolution will be steadily carried out. We shall regenerate in this land the high renaissance of our forefathers. We shall continue our untiring effort to preserve our pride in being a cultured nation, with the inherited ideals of *hongik ingan* and the spirit of *hwarang-do,* by fully developing the talents of our people.

a quiet
revolution

The eventful 1960's, which will be recorded as one of the most stirring and memorable decades in our history, have come to an end.

We reached a turning point early in the last decade as the people were awakened, began to realize their creative power, and united to work for the resurrection of their nation. During the eight or nine years since then we have concentrated all our efforts on the task of modernization of our country, and have reaped many dividends.

Thus today the whole world looks upon our people with respect and admiration, in a new recognition that the wartorn Korea of the 1950's has now emerged as an exemplary model for the development of emerging countries. Rather than the visible accomplishment itself, what I think most valuable is the rediscovery, in the process of this achievement, of the limitless power of our people, and our newly-won pride and confidence that we can accomplish any great task through our own will and effort.

We have now entered the 1970's, the decade when we must achieve without fail the national resurrection which began in the sixties.

The seeds of our future have been sown, and the first buds are beginning to sprout. At such a time the responsibility of leadership becomes all the heavier. Yet history is not made by leaders alone. Leaders are but the catalysts, the stimulants to growth.

One can liken our national ideals to seeds. Only when the seed is good and carefully fertilized will the land bear fruit. Just as flowers wither, a people can become poor without good leadership.

Similarly, good ideals and leadership can only be utilized by a receptive people. And in the last analysis, the soil can supply its own nutrients so that plants can at least survive. The people, like the soil, are the ultimate masters.

The people and their leadership must become of one mind in marching toward their goal, so that planned national changes can be made, and new, unplanned progress awakened and pursued spontaneously. Backed by the fervor of a united people, its leadership must take the initiative and set the example.

In the course of advancing toward our ideals, conflicting views and opinions are bound to arise and national opinion may be divided. Although competition and constructive criticism are a necessary source of fresh creation and reform, we should abstain from the kind of division that is excessive, unproductive, or aimless. All of us must keep our sense of direction if we are to meet the rapid changes and reforms that are bound to take place. To this end, we must further a realistic dialogue between leadership and the people, sharing their common feelings. In so doing we uphold the democracy which we have accepted, and which has taken root deep in our national consciousness.

What should Koreans hope and plan to accomplish during the coming decade? Above all, we must achieve a completely self-sufficient economy. Our per capita income should far exceed five hundred dollars. Our export volume should go beyond the five billion dollar mark. Every aspect of our national economy, including its scale, should be enhanced to a level whereby it can be evaluated favorably on an international standard. The quality of our manufactured goods should be so high that they prevail over those of other advanced nations in the international market. We should concentrate on manufacturing a number of products in which we can take pride in their being the best in the world.

Accomplishing these goals will require unusually painstaking efforts in many fields. A rapid development of science and technology and of management techniques demands our immediate attention and should be given top priority. Thus we should achieve our national development to such an extent as to earn Korea a spot at the top of the developing countries of the world.

In order to do this, we must speed up construction of highway systems and the comprehensive development of the entire land to make possible the transportation of people and commodities throughout the country in one

The Honam Fertilizer Plant
at Naju was completed and began
production of urea fertilizer in 1962,
preceded by the Chungju Plant in 1960.
Today, there are five
urea fertilizer plants in Korea in addition
to three other chemical fertilizer plants.

day's time. We must further develop and expand our harbor facilities and sea transportation networks to handle an annual average of ten billion dollars' worth of goods.

We must also carry out a balanced regional development program to bridge the gap between rural and urban areas. We must work hard to help farmers convert the roofs of their houses from thatch to tile. We must create enough jobs for all the people and make one person's wage sufficient to support a family, thereby providing a comfortable level of subsistence for the people.

All of us must work together closely, united in our aims if these goals are to be attained. We should rid ourselves of the tendency to view others with jealousy and suspicion. We should also give up the idea of gaining profit for ourselves by corrupt practices. A clean, honest and pleasant social climate is a prerequisite for the realization of our goals.

Culture and art, as the purifiers of our national consciousness and of our society, should be applied more closely to our daily lives. A sound national spirit formed by the popularization of wholesome family-level recreation and national sports should serve as the foundation of our strength as a nation.

In the political arena, we should discard extremism and violent struggle. Instead, we must foster constructive discussion and competition, thereby reaping the fruits of true democracy.

In the seventies we must search positively for means of national reunification. We should constantly maintain a position of power overwhelmingly superior to that of the North Korean Communists so that we can immediately and effectively deal with or respond to any reunification plan, be it peaceful or non-peaceful. We should always maintain a self-reliant defense capability strong enough to enable us to crush by ourselves any aggression launched solely by the North Korean Communists. This is what I mean by the spirit of independence, self-reliance and self-help, of which I have so often spoken.

We must continue with our peaceful efforts for national reunification to the very end. But we must be prepared to meet force with force.

I would like to emphasize the importance of self-reliance in our own defense. The primary responsibility for Korea's defense falls on our own shoulders. If we rely on others for our national defense without having a strong determination and thorough preparedness to defend ourselves from aggression, we will be inviting grave misfortune.

Korea will always be grateful to the 16 allies who promptly came to its aid when the North Korean Communists started the Korean War. We believe that the United States, our great ally in peace and war, will come to our aid if we are invaded from without. There is no doubt about this in view of the traditionally close ties of friendship between the two countries and the underlying spirit of the Korean-American Mutual Defense Treaty. We must remember, however, that support and assistance from allies will neither be forthcoming nor be of any substantial help until and unless we have made deserving efforts of our own to defend ourselves.

Above all, we need to further strengthen our determination and ability to achieve self-sufficiency in all

*The then Mayor
of West Berlin, Willy Brandt,
greets the author
when the latter visited
that divided "island" city
in December, 1964.
Looking over to the other
side of the Berlin Wall,
the author felt:
"I now see North Korea
through East Berlin."*

areas. We must do our very best to establish a self-reliant defense posture and forge a formidable military might that the Communists will respect. But we must also concentrate our efforts and resources on national development. We must discourage the North Korean Communists from harboring any aggressive intent by securing a position of absolute supremacy over them economically, culturally, militarily, and otherwise. Such self-reliance in economy and defense is a mighty deterrent against war, a shortcut to unification, and the path to prosperity and peace for our fifty million people.

Let me emphasize that we must realize all these tasks in the 1970's. If we succeed in doing so, we shall have finished most of the tasks involved in the modernization of our country within a single decade. The goals and plans we have for the seventies are not mere speculation. Given our country's wisdom and strength, it will not be too hard to attain them. They might even be attainable with considerably less endeavor than that which has been required of us in overcoming all the adverse situations we have experienced so far.

Nothing new or unusual is required. I believe that we can easily accomplish our goals if we continue to work steadily and substantially with the same passion, industry and effort that we have demonstrated during the last several years. We must eliminate promptly the remaining unproductive habits we have carried over from the past if we are to be successful in realizing our goals.

It has been about a quarter of a century since Korea's liberation after World War II. We might well keep in mind that in another 25 years or so this century will be close to its end. No one can predict precisely what the world will be like around the year 2000, or where the Republic of Korea will stand at that time.

Nevertheless, our country by then ought to have become a strong nation-state, having achieved unification long before. It should have become an affluent and advanced welfare state, with everyone enjoying prosperity; it should have become a respected, participating member of the international community, contributing to the annals of world history.

Now is the time for steady preparation. Thus the present decade, which links the past with the future in our modern history, is a critical period in which the success or failure of the national resurrection will be determined. The achievement of national resurrection in this decade depends upon whether we can mobilize our resources for productive purposes.

The keys to national resurrection are the mobilization of resources and national unity. It is only national unity that will ensure the attainment of our immediate goals: a self-sustaining national economy and a self-reliant national defense. It is also our strength of unity that will eventually achieve the national aspiration of unification of our divided country.

Monumental tasks lie ahead. During the 1970's, our decade of greatest hope, we will have to shift our main thrust from economic to social development. This effort will begin with the third five-year economic plan, to be launched in 1972 on successful attainment of the first and second plans. Our progress must spread evenly

throughout society if we are to attain a happy, prosperous commonwealth.

We will continue in our steady, quiet revolution, founded in democracy. With a joy born of achievement, we will prove that this invisible revolution of ours has something greater than anything that preceded it. While the revolution is ripening within, we can find joy in our realization that our national foundations have become solid.

We must not and will not throw away this rare opportunity. We will continue to march forward courageously in the firm belief that our national revival will contribute to humanity's progress, remembering always that we will be unable to participate in mankind's advance unless we first command our own national destiny. Those who give up halfway to their goals can never win. Those who emerge as victors never give up.

REPUBLIC OF KOREA

CHINA

SEATTLE

HONG KONG
SEOUL
TAIPEI
TOKYO
SAN FRANCISCO

HAWAII

CHINA

Tumen River

N. HAMKYONG
PROVINCE

Najin

2541
▲ Mt. Paektu

Chongjin

2541
▲ Kwanmo Bong

Yalu River

Kanggye

S. HAMKYONG
PROVINCE

N. PYONGAN
PROVINCE

Songjin

Antung

Chang-chon River

40°

Sinuiju   Sonchon

Hamhung

Taedong River

S. PYONGAN
PROVINCE

Kowon

Tonghan Bay

Yangdok

Yonghung Bay

EAST S

Pyongyang

Wonsan

1638

▲ Mt. Kumgang

Sariwon

38°

HWANGHAE PROVINCE

Imjin River

Kosong

Cholwon

Sokcho

Haeju

Uijongbu

KANG WON PROVINCE

DMZ

Han River

Seoul

Kangnung

Inchon

Wonju

YELLOW SEA

KYONGKI PROVINCE

Mt. Taebaek
▲

Ullung

N. CHUNGCHONG
PROVINCE

Chonan
Chongju

Chomchon Andong

Yongil Bay

36°

S. CHUNGCHONG
PROVINCE

Taejon

N. KYONGSANG PROVINCE

Kunsan

I-Ri

Kimchon

Pohang

Chunju

Taegu

Kyongju

Nakdong River

1915
▲ Mt. Chiri

S. KYONGSANG
PROVINCE

N. CHOLLA PROVINCE

Kwangju

Masan Pusan

Chinju

Mokpo

Sunchon

Korea Strait

34°

S. CHOLLA PROVINCE

JAPAN

125°

Cheju Strait

Scale of Kilo

0

Cheju

CHEJU PROVINCE
▲ 1950
Mt. Halla

◎ Capital

International Boundaries

○ Cities

Provincial Boundaries

index

a

Admiral Yi Sunshin 24
Alphabet 24, 39, 48, 190
American Revolution 38
An Chang Ho 50
An Jaehong 65
An Jungkeun 51
Anglo-Russian Rivalry 32
Arabs 21
Armistice (cease-fire) 82, 86,
 102, 135, 152
Asia 21, 35, 136, 146, 147
Asian and Pacific Council
 (ASPAC) 139
Australia 160

b

Berlin, city of 150
Bible 39
Boxer Rebellion 35
Britain, Great 36, 50
British Fleet 33
Buddhism 22, 42, 54
Bumindan 53
Byrnes, James E. 71

c

Cambodia 149, 160
Canada 160
Chang Myon (John M. Chang)
 95
Charter of National Education
 132
Ceylon 158
Chang Jiyeon 50
Chile 160

Ch'ing (dynasty) 20, 22;
 China 33, 35, 136
Chistiakov, Lt. Gen. I. M. 69
China, Republic of 157
China, Communist 78, 79, 82,
 146, 147, 152; Soviet aid to
 80
Chollado Province 42
Chondo-gyo (religion) 54
Chosun Ilbo (newspaper) 60
Christianity 38, 39, 42, 54
Communism 13, 63, 85, 129,
 131, 147, 167
Confucianism 22, 38, 39, 42, 107
Construction Ministry 126
Czechoslovakia 56

d

Democratic Party 95, 96, 102,
 104, 105
Development Loan Fund (DLF)
 91
Diplomatic Missions: Africa 129;
 Latin America 129; Middle
 East 129; Southwest Asia 129
Dong-a Ilbo (newspaper) 60

e

Economic Planning Board 126
Economy, Korean 14, 29, 91,
 97, 99, 101, 102, 104, 105,
 107, 108, 110, 111, 113, 114,
 116, 117, 120, 123, 127, 129,
 131, 134, 139, 172, 173, 176,
 179, 181, 182, 184, 187, 199,
 204

Education, Korean 88, 89, 124,
127, 130, 132, 166, 182;
Charter of National Education
185
Egypt 56
Eisenhower, Dwight D. 83
Elections, general 18, 72, 74,
75, 78, 94, 152, 153, 161, 163
Encyclopedia Britannica 17
Exports, Korean 30, 108, 117,
120, 173, 175, 199
Expressways: Seoul-Pusan, 120,
121; Seoul-Inchon 120; Taejon-
Chonju 121
"Extended Central Committee
of the Democratic Front for
National Unification" 78

f

"Fatherland Unification Demo-
cratic Front" 161
Five-Year Plan: First Five-Year
Plan 107, 108, 110, 113, 123,
124, 203; Second Five-Year
Plan 114, 123, 124, 203; Third
Five-Year Plan 175, 203
Foreign Aid 88, 91, 102, 104, 127
Foreign Operations Administra-
tion (FOA) 91
France 35, 160
French Revolution 38

g

Gabo Kyongjang 45, 47
Geneva, city of 158

Geneva Political Conference 152
Germany, Federal Republic of
176
Ghandi, Mahatma 59
Gangwa Treaty 35
Gapsin Political Incident 41, 42,
44, 47
Gojong, Emperor 48
Gromyko, Andrei 72
Gross National Product (GNP)
29, 108, 116, 120
Gutenberg 24

h

Haeju 79
Han Dynasty 20, 22
Hangul (alphabet) 24, 39, 48, 190
Heungsadan Movement 50, 53
Hideyoshi 21
Hirobumi Ito 51
Hodge, Lt. Gen. John R. 66, 69
Hongik Ingan 24, 25, 26, 182,
185, 187
Hwangguk Hyophoe (Imperial
Association 50
hwarang 24, 25, 187
hwarang-do 25
Hwarangdo chongsin 25

i

Il-sung, Kim 69, 72, 75, 78, 136,
161, 163, 164, 166, 167
unification proposal 161

Inchon, city of 65, 80
Independence Association 95
India 56, 59
Indochina 139
Indonesia 158
Industrial Revolution 38
Industry, Korean 102, 104, 108,
    110, 111, 113, 116, 121, 175,
    176, 181
International Cooperation
    Agency (ICA) 91
Invasions 20, 21, 25, 28, 38, 77,
    78, 135, 136
Iraq 158
Ireland 56
Islam 21

J

Japan 20, 21, 33, 35, 41, 42, 44,
    45, 47, 50, 51, 53, 57, 59, 60,
    63, 65, 94, 129, 130, 136, 146,
    176; surrender of 28
Japanese: annexation of Korea
    51, 56; surrender of troops 63;
    samurai 25
Jeon Bongjun 42

 K

Kaehwa Tongnip Party (The
    Independence Club) 41, 42
Kaesong 79
Khitan 20
Kim Koo 69
Kim Okgyun 41, 42
Kinkaid, Admiral Thomas C. 66
Kobu 42

Koguryo, Kingdom of 18
Kojong, King 42, 112
Komun Island (Port Hamilton)
    32, 33
Korea, North 68, 69, 72, 75, 78,
    79, 82, 96, 144, 146, 153, 158,
    160, 161, 164, 166, 167, 178;
    army 79; defense treaty with
    Red China 78; people's com-
    mittee 69, 71, 75; population
    21; Soviet occupation of 68
Korea, South 72, 74, 75, 78, 79,
    96, 152, 158, 160, 161, 163,
    164
Korean: independence 14, 33,
    45, 53, 54, 56, 57, 59; libera-
    tion 51, 60, 63, 85, 132; mili-
    tary 14; population 21, 29, 92,
    102, 116, 153; partition 19;
    reunification 74, 77, 78, 80,
    99, 150, 152, 157, 161, 164,
    166, 167, 169, 201, 202, 205
Korean Institute of Science and
    Technology 29
Korean-Japanese Relations 57,
    146
Korean-U.S. Mutual Defense
    Treaty 83, 202
Korean-U.S. Relations 146
Korean Language Society 60
Korean Students Conference on
    Independence 53
Korean War 13, 82, 83, 85, 86,
    88, 95, 131, 146, 150, 160, 161,
    164, 166, 191, 202; armistice
    (cease-fire) 82, 86, 102, 135,
    136; casualties 83; refugees 88;
    proposals for settlement 152,
    153

Koryo, dynasty 20, 22, 24

Labor Unions 105
Laos 149
Liaotung Peninsula 35
Liberal Party 28, 89, 94, 97, 99,
    102, 104, 110, 129
Lovett, Robert A. 72

MacArthur, Gen. Douglas 66,
    79, 80, 82
Malik, Jakob 82
Manchu 20, 38
Manchuria 35, 53, 59, 60, 78,
    82, 136
Mao Tse-tung 80
Marshall (Secretary of State) 72
Martial law 130
Masan 94
Military or Revolutionary
    Government 105, 107, 126,
    127, 129
Military Revolution 28, 29, 97,
    101, 127
Min Yeonghwan 50
Ming Dynasty 22
Modernization, Korean 38, 41,
    42, 44, 45, 47, 48, 50, 51, 54,
    62, 88, 95, 99, 111, 121, 124,
    127, 131, 138, 179, 182, 184,
    197, 204

Molotov 71, 72
Mongols 19, 136
Mongolia 22
Moscow 71, 78, 153
Mutual Security Act (U. S.) 91

Nathan Report 110
National Assembly 75
NATO 144
New Zealand 160
Nixon, Richard M. 144; doctrine
    144, 146, 147

Office of National Tax Admin-
    istration 126

Pacific War 136
Pakchae, Kingdom of 20
Pakistan 160
Panmunjom 96, 150
Parallel, 38th 63, 66, 69, 79, 80
Peaceful Co-existence 91, 141
Peking, city of 78, 80
Poland 56
Press 50, 53, 105, 127, 166
Potsdam Declaration 65
Preparatory Committee for
    Nation-Building 65, 66

Provisional Government-in-Exile
(Korean) 59, 69, 95
Pusan 30, 80
Pyongyang 69, 161

r

Reform, Korean 39, 41, 44, 45,
48, 50, 51, 101, 126, 127
Rhee, Syngman 50, 69, 75, 77,
82, 89, 99, 102
Republic of Korea, constitution
75
Roosevelt, Theodore 36
Russian Army 68
Russian Occupation forces 69
Russo-Japanese War 36, 136

s

Samil Independence Movement
27
Seoul 24, 48, 65, 69, 78, 80, 94,
139, 150
Sejong, King (the Great) 24
Seventh Fleet 66
Shanghai 53, 59, 95
Shimonoseki Treaty 35
Sil-Hak (School of Practical
Science) 22, 38, 39
Silla, Kingdom of 20; Silla
Dynasty 20, 22, 24, 25, 27
Sino-Japanese War 35, 136
Sohak (Western Learning) 42
Sokkuram Stone Cave Temple 25

Son Byeonghi 54
Song Jinwu 65
Songrihak 187
Soviet Union (or Russia) 33, 35,
50, 65, 72, 78, 79, 136, 141,
143, 152, 157
Stalin, Josef 80
Stevenson, Adlai 158
Students 28, 94, 101, 105, 129,
132, 163
Sui Dynasty 20
Sung Dynasty 22

t

T'ang culture 22; dynasty 20
Tangun 25
Taoism 42
Thailand 158
The Hague, city of 51
The Hague Peace Conference 51
"Third World" 143, 157
Tonghak (chondo-gyo) religion
42, 44
Tonghak Revolution 41, 42, 44,
47, 48, 50
Tongnip Hyophoe (Independence
Association) 47, 48, 50
Tongnip Shinmun (The Inde-
pendent) 48
Truman, Harry S 79, 80
Trusteeship Plan 71
Tumen River 82
Tunisia 158
Turkey 56, 160

U

Ulsa Treaty 51
Ulsan 121
United Nations 72, 75, 82, 114,
    152, 153, 157, 158, 164, 166;
    military assistance 79; forces
    79, 80, 82, 152, 160; Korea's
    admission 157
U.N. Commission for the Uni-
    fication and Rehabilitation of
    Korea 157, 158
U.N. General Assembly 72, 74,
    75, 77, 152, 153, 158, 160
U.N. Korean Reconstruction
    Agency 157
U.N. Security Council 79, 157
U.N. Temporary Commission on
    Korea 74, 75, 77
United States 47, 53, 65, 71, 74,
    77, 82, 117, 141, 143. 144,
    146, 147, 149, 172, 202;
    economic aid 83, 91, 104;
    military assistance 77; military
    government 69; troops 65, 83,
    135, 163, 185
U.S. Joint Chiefs of Staff 80
U.S. Public Law 480 (1953) 91
USS Pueblo 166

V

Vietnam 131, 144, 147, 149, 172
Vietnam, North 147, 152

Vietnam War 139, 147, 149; Paris
    negotiations 147; ROK troops
    in 131, 139

W

Wake Island 80
Warsaw Pact 144
Woodrow Wilson 56
World War I 53, 56, 59
World War II 18, 28, 57, 136

Y

Yalu River 82
Yang Youchan Dr. 83
Yeo Wunheong 65
Yeongjo, King 21
Yi Dynasty 20, 22, 23, 25, 38,
    59, 187
Yi Hwang (Toige) 38
Yi I (Yulgok) 38
Yi Jun 51
Yi Korea 107, 127
Yi Sangjae 48
Yonghung Bay (Port Lagarett) 33
Yuan 20, 22
Yugoslavia 56
Yun Chiho 48